IT CAN TURN

Dr Zikhona Hlalempini

ISBN: 978-1-991218-92-6 (Print)

Illustrator:
Motsanaphe Morare (MoMaLifeLiving.com)

Editor and Proof-reader:
Luyanda Thela (ldlamini@thegoldengooseinstitute.com)

I would love to hear from you. Your questions, your
comments are welcome. Don't be a stranger. My contact
information is listed below, and I encourage you to contact
me. I am also available for speaking engagements.

My email address is zikhona7@yahoo.com

This book was published by
The Golden Goose Institute (Pty) Ltd

For further information email:
info@thegoldengooseinstitute.com

DEDICATION

I humbly dedicate this book to my mother
in Heaven and to my four children on earth.
It is dedicated to all who seek to rise above their pain
into a future filled with multiple possibilities.

ACKNOWLEDGEMENTS

I am not sure why I had such an urge to write, but one thing was recurring—the passing of time. I felt that my experiences would make a difference if shared and that many would be inspired to be better. It is now time to live more intentional lives. I knew that if I wrote too early it would be too soon and if wrote too late I would forget the critical things I wanted to say, thus the time is now. It is the time the Lord has declared.

I would like to thank God, the Almighty, who felt it imperative that I should teach the gospel of lives turning, of situations turning, of remembering our identities and pursuing our purposes—whatever the cost. The gospel of dreams and believing in ourselves. Some people would term it betting on yourself. You are the winning horse, you are the Powerball. There is no greater choice than the one we can all individually make to change the world. The power lies in us, the human race. May my story remind you of the importance of dreaming and remaining true to who you are. May your dreams continually scare you.

My beautiful mother Ncumisa Hlalempini who continues to be the wind at my back and a constant beckoning of hope to become more than I can ever be. You are alive for as long as I still stand. I love you and honour your beautiful life always. I had you in mind throughout the writing of this book.

I would like to give thanks to the family that taught me independence and the responsibility that lies in the choices we make.

I thank you, uncle Vusumzi, for poems and books and for translating what was being said on our television from English to Xhosa. That kind of care experienced as a child made me feel important. I can now describe it as giving me self-worth.

My two living aunts, Sisi Ayanda and Sisi Sindiswa thank you for weathering the storms with me and teaching me about the value of family, even with my mother gone.

My aunt, Sisi Phumeza, alongside my mother in Heaven. Thank you for being my mother's best friend and choosing to depart with her so that she is not lonely on the other side. The beautiful dishes you made for me and my family and all the copious sacrifices you made for us will never be forgotten.

Acknowledgements

My children Aza, Luthi, Lwalwa, Emma—thank you for the magic you provide to me daily. I still stand in awe every time I watch the four of you. Thank you for choosing me to be your mother. Remember that our bond will last till the end of time.

Dr Onke Tshiki—thank you for choosing me as your soulmate. It has been two decades of love, fights, learning, tears, calm, storms, providing, parenting, and most importantly eternal admiration. Your genius still takes my breath away. Thank you for making Medical School bearable.

Grant Senzani—you took a chance on a stranger and in that process turned me into an author. Thank you for seeing and believing in my vision. Thank you for our Zoom chats and all the ideas shared about changing the world. I respect your ideologies and your vision to turn even the man walking on the street into an author. I look forward to many collaborations together. Thank you for helping push this precious baby into the world. This book belongs to both of us.

Luyanda Thela—your grace and the eloquent manner in which you live your life is unmatched. Words are a territory that you rule—a world entirely of your own. I am so grateful I got to meet and know you even before we started working together. I still stand at the door and wonder how people like you were made. What kind of genetic material must have been mixed to produce such a captivating soul? Thank you.

Nombuyiselo Hlalempini—thank you for having my back throughout our childhood. Thank you for not leaving too soon. You stayed long enough for me to process your passing. My children have lost an aunt in you. May you continue to watch over us and rest in peace, my beautiful cousin. Your life was one of a kind and we who loved you remember you each day.

CONTENTS

THE THORN BIRDS[1]

By Colleen McCullough

"There is a legend about a bird which sings only once in its life, more beautiful than any other creature on the face of the earth. From the moment it leaves its nest it searches for a thorn tree and does not rest until it has found one. Then, it impales its breast on the longest, sharpest thorn. But as it is dying, it rises above its own agony to out sing the Lark and the Nightingale. The Thorn bird pays its life for that one song, and the whole world stills to listen, and God in his heaven smiles, as its best is brought only at the cost of great pain; Driven to the thorn with no knowledge of the dying to come. But we, when we press the thorn to our breasts, we know. We understand. And still, we do it. Still we do it."

"It's the fact that I've, or rather, we've fizzled out. Pretty soon now The Hlalempinis will be no more. Oh no, they will give us a line in the history books and say here lived thinkers. But none of you will ever know anything about us. You should have been one of us, yes, lest you were one of us"

—**Vusumzi Hlalempini**

INTRODUCTION

Apocalypse
By Emily Dickinson[2]

I'm wife; I've finished that,
That other state;
I'm Czar, I'm woman now:
It's safer so.

How odd the girl's life looks
Behind this soft eclipse!
I think that earth seems so
To those in heaven now.

This being comfort, then
That other kind was pain;
But why compare?
I'm wife! Stop there!

I have never been quite the same following the end of my marriage in the winter of 2016, in a small South African town called East London. I am still uncertain whether it was just because of the circumstances surrounding the rapidly dying marriage or whether it was the temperature, but that remains the worst winter I have ever experienced. My heart was freezing and I'm not sure whether any diagnosis and treatment plan was available for my perceived dying self—heart and all. The core of my sense of being had been shaken so horribly that I was left without an identity. Being stripped of the title "wife" felt literal—something had been forcibly and physically taken away from me. When checking into a hotel, my husband would politely ask for a room for him and his wife. Those moments were filled with such delicious gentleness and adoration, him carrying our bags to our room and our tradition of watching re-runs of *Friends*—we were addicted.

If I was not his wife then, who was I? I felt like a displaced alien, out of touch with my real home, stuck in an overcrowded filthy planet whose language I did not speak. I had no idea that my mind's connections had become so underground, even to me, like a deep dark wide web of some sort. My mind had stopped identifying me as an individual. It had replaced me with wife and once wife was deleted, permanently so, I was also permanently deleted. It is also interesting to note the message of the above poem written by Emily Dickinson, who was never married. The poem talks about the completeness that marriage offers. This was something that had always been desired, even in the nineteenth century. Spinsters like Emily and her sister, who were required to look after their parents, seemed to have longed for this. When I read it clearly and breathe as I read it, my heart has palpitations that make me cry.

It felt as though I had been erased from the face of the earth, yet I was present. A shadow of my former self, *ghost-like,* as a well-meaning best friend once described me. I lived and breathed for this title and wearing that ring every day was an affirmation that I belonged to someone, that I had achieved something. I had not yet learnt that achieving permanent things with another person is like building pies in the sky. Those things remain true if the person you built them with continues to want to build with you. Without that ring, it was so difficult to return to me. Even my name, given to me at birth, was suddenly meaningless. Didn't the universe know that I was a Mrs? That any other title would simply not suffice?

The aftermath of the end of my marriage reminded me often of falling. There was often this imagery of falling into a bottomless pit. I would sometimes wake up drenched in sweat from this perpetual nightmare. I would try to lull myself back to sleep like a baby—that's how fragile I had become.

There was even more complex imagery that will last my entire lifetime. Around the time when my marriage was ending, there was a popular black racing driver who passed away during a summit to Kilimanjaro. His name was Gugu Zulu. I had never known him before this devastating news. I learnt so much about him as his story unfolded. I remember reading the story as his devastated and grieving wife, Letshego Zulu, recalled the bruises they suffered as they came down that gigantic mountain. The story she told became a personal mantra and a prayer for me as I was losing my husband. She describes, in harrowing detail, how they tried to bring her husband to safety and to care. You realise the brilliance, beauty, and bravery of her story when she talks about the descent. It was her final dance with her beloved husband, even though she may not have realised it then. It is filled with contrasts. There is an extreme love for her dying husband and a difficult descent with a guide on unfamiliar terrain. Her story pieced together the first innate layers of my fractured psyche. I knew that I would never be the same and there was a lot to come, but I prayed for so much strength.

My prayer would start something like this, "Heavenly Father, I know this is the season for my fall. My prayer is this: as I descend this gigantic mountain ahead of me may you guide me. May I fall with grace. May you heal my bruises, lacerations, and fractures as I come down. May you guide my descent whether financial, mental, spiritual, or emotional. May you help me come down this mountain carrying my children. May their bruises be on my very body because they did nothing to suddenly wake up without a family anymore, or rather one that had been redefined and restructured almost overnight." I never asked to not be bruised, to not be lacerated, or to not be fractured. I merely asked for help to endure it well because I knew that I could not have prepared for what I was about to experience.

We had a great marriage. We loved each other immensely, intensely, and completely. We had beautiful children, a beautiful home, but it was not meant to be. I was not lucky enough, even with all those lovely ingredients. In another small way, I was lucky. As an avid reader and historian, I had an understanding that very few things last forever. I have read many stories of empires that had risen, were overthrown, and continued to rise again. The Bible itself is a fitting example of this. The Northern Kingdom of Israel was captured by Assyria which was also captured by the Babylonians who were overthrown without any bloodshed because their king had seen the writing on the wall the night before Cyrus came for them. He went on to become master of entire western Asia. The types of transitions of Cyrus of the Medes may still echo today. And as raw as my pain was at this time, I had a prayer that my loss would eventually lead me to peace and eventually to meaning.

In her book of essays, Jane Yolen[3] writes that "Literature is a textually transmitted disease, normally contracted in childhood." Here she describes me unequivocally. When I was younger, all I ever wanted to do was read and write. I was lucky because I had a genius of an uncle who instilled this seed in me. I looked up to him because he was like a dictionary. He knew the meaning of every word that I asked him. He was among the students chosen by some American initiative to study at the prestigious All Saints High School and this led to him moving to a boarding school. Even though we are eleven years apart, we have always been very close. We would reread and recall from memory his favourite poems that in time became our favourites too. Even though I lived in a township, my mother would save enough money for me to go to the library every Saturday, and that is where I fell in love with the scent of books.

There is always a book on my nightstand. During the first few years after my marriage ended, I always slept with a copy of *A grief observed* by C. S. Lewis; I must have had ten copies. How I longed to have been loved the way C. S. Lewis loved H. I will never believe that any woman could have ever been loved that much till the end of time.

Reading and writing have been my two idiosyncrasies from around the age of eight. My mom would encourage me and would buy me A4 books to continue my writing. I had fallen in love with words and this relationship would last my entire life. Literature, paragraphs, and verses by my favourite authors have kept me alive. Let me reiterate this in case you had not read that emphatically enough: words have kept me alive.

I had always known that I would also author a book. A book that resembled those written by my heroes; Sylvia Plath, Virginia Woolf, Ernest Hemingway, WH Auden, TS Elliot, Ted Hughes, WB Yeats, Alfred Lord Tennyson, Ingrid Jonker, Marguerite Poland, Harper Lee, and an infinite number of other authors. I never in a million years envisaged writing this kind of book—one in which I would bear my soul. I had an idea that I would be like Truman Capote and would write one enjoyable book and that would be the end, just as he wrote *In cold blood*. The world would have heard my message and that is all I would have wanted. Again, it is in books that I found comfort, in the words of Sylvia Plath[4] who stated that everything in life is writable about if you have the outgoing guts to do it, and the imagination to improvise. The worst enemy to creativity is self-doubt.

This is a book about the end of a marriage which I adored, worshipped, and loved. A marriage that replaced the parts of God that lived within me because I had decided that it would fulfil the roles of a deity. How very wrong my assumptions were. This led to the death of my hope for love and the beginning of my struggles with my mental health while juggling being a full-time parent to four children. The book is also about the courage of my mother as she dealt with a new me. She often told me her daughter died when the marriage ended but what I loved about my feisty mother was that she was there for even this person she did not recognise. I never knew that a person could disappear without being reported as missing until I disappeared in front of everyone's eyes. Everything that defined me had been lost, and so it was that I was also lost. The book also deals with other life experiences traversed in my journey and I try throughout the book to leave messages of hope.

This book will illustrate how prevalent mental health challenges are and the statistics will scare you. The desperate acts of a demented mind will provoke you to see how no one else should go through all that I've been through. If only I had prioritised my truths before chasing titles. If only I had tweaked myself and my dreams less, there would have been some hope for me. But after all the tweaking and pleasing and not living my true self, my mind attacked, and the attack almost cost me my life.

I want you to be clear that your ideas of who you want to be matter. That chasing your identity and who you want to be matters. You matter. Resilience is developed through time like a survival instinct, or adrenaline awaiting to be unleashed. Resilience comes in the morning, as long as we are standing, for as long as we remain standing, it is a gift for us all. Like the Athenians of old, let us die standing not kneeling, and not lying on a bed. The Athenians died standing while fighting for their lives, and not kneeling in defeat.

The message of this book is that of finding an identity of your own—not one forged by parents, lovers, friends, or religion. All these people and institutions are transient. You live with yourself for the rest of your life. The next powerful message is one of meaning. Finding meaning in the chaos, in a time and place where nothing seems like it will ever make sense. I implore you to be wiser than I have been. Find your voice by first being honest to yourself about who you are and where you want to go. Do not minimise or tweak your dreams and your story just to please another.

This book contains truths about my life and the reasons behind the decisions I made. I felt it important that my shortcomings and short-sightedness be made public to the world so that the generations that will follow may be wiser and better prepared for the challenges that life imposes, even if those challenges are from the people we love most in the world. This book will show you that it's okay to be weak, to struggle, or to not be okay. Life contains challenges—and it must—that's the only way that we can expect to grow. If we embrace the impermanence of situations and persons in our lives, we will enjoy a more purposeful life.

As a 40-year-old, I have had an immense amount of time over the years to find out what truths could assist me in the pursuit of finding my identity. I have studied Christianity, Judaism, Buddhism, African roots, and the diverse types of healers and rituals of many diverse cultures. I have chosen the bits that resonate and speak to me. I read and practice the knowledge learnt that continues to change my life. I believe in the power of meditation and the power of continual self-cleansing and alignment of energies and chakras. This book is written to expand, not only knowledge about yourself but knowledge about the world.

INDIGENOUS GAMES
Hoola Hoops

INDIGENOUS GAMES
Ingxowa Yetyiwa

INDIGENOUS GAMES
Puca

INDIGENOUS GAMES
Sdudla Khalipha

INDIGENOUS GAMES
Ugqaphu

CHAPTER 1:

MY CHILDHOOD

"All grown-ups were once children...
but only few remember it"
—Antoine de Saint-Exupery, The Little Prince

My mother's name was Ncumisa Hlalempini. Ncumisa means someone who can make others smile. She always reminded me of the quote by Dr Seuss, "Adults are just absolute children and the hell with them." I am not sure whether my mother ever grew up. She was the happiest person I had ever met, with a smile and a laugh that resembled that of a child. She had that gift given to her a thousand-fold. Even writing about her in the past tense is painful. She was the most alive person that I had ever met. I have never seen her hold or read a book: it was as though she was allergic to them. She read only for her teaching diploma and her degree. She was a genius who asked me to read for her and that was enough for her to go and write exams. She was the third of five children, born when her parents had a white wedding. She used to say this often, it seemed important to her. She had amazing parents and when she spoke about her father who had passed away when she was ten, it felt like she had seen him just the day before.

Her father's incredible treatment of her mother ruined her for other men. None would have compared to her father. Some tried, but just never got it right. She was born in Lloyd Street, East London. Her family members were then forcefully relocated to the newly built townships during the apartheid era. This move was part of the implementation of the Group Areas Act of 1950. It enforced racial segregation in East London and South Africa as a whole. The removals and resettlements began in the same year that the building of the township began, in 1963. By 1966 Mdantsane became a homeland town under Ciskei. To further manipulate people into leaving their homes and ways of life, the Regional Industrial Development Programme (RIDP) was enacted. Here, various factories were built as close to Mdantsane as possible to encourage people to move with an incentive. This sounds like a perfect solution on paper, but the low wages and lack of funding of the programme by the 1990s as well as trade unions opened the pandora's box. The dreams, sold to many, were lost in a puff of smoke.

This remains a painful memory as people were uprooted from their lives into townships and houses that were four-roomed for an entire family—no matter how big the family was. Some people were asked to temporarily share this four-roomed house with another family. Imagine sharing a bathroom with another family for your entire lifetime? They were promised houses as soon as they became available, and these were two-roomed houses.

My family established a home in Mdantsane township. My grandmother, Rivha, was a housewife and her husband was a Swallows former rugby player and rugby coach and the provider for their family of seven. My grandparents lost two sets of twins, which was a devastating loss, but still, they continued as a family. My mother had only the best memories of her childhood, even after their father was murdered in front of them by the family that lived across the street from them. He was murdered over children's quarrels. My grandmother took over the care of the family along with her firstborn who also joined the factory where my grandmother worked. My grandmother eventually became part of the management team at the factory.

My mother was a naughty child. She invented new ways of making my grandmother age long before her time along with her only brother, Vusumzi, who seemed to go along with my mother's antics. My mother grew up in an era when certain things were meant only for adults. For instance, if on a particular day they had samp and beans for supper (staple food for most people at the time), the children would have to eat their meal with Holsum and salt while my gran would have delicious things to go with her meal like Aromat, margarine and other spices. My mother would find a way to ensure that she also ate her samp and beans with style—spices and all.

My mother and uncle were often in trouble. I can imagine my gran reminding her that she was older and should know better. She enjoyed sharing a story of how when she would come across a bar of chocolate while pretending to be cleaning granny's room, she would eat it and find a pin to make markings on the packaging so that it seemed like a rat had eaten the chocolate. She would also pretend that she didn't eat the things that she enjoyed just so that when they disappeared from the fridge, she would not be a suspect. This was always a one-man job and mom would not tell a soul. She would watch people eating custard and not eat it, but when no one was looking, she would devour it.

My mother loved her mother. She spoke often and in detail about her mother's last days and the conversations they had. My gran had a second stroke, and my mom took care of her. We would take turns changing her. This was easy for my mom to do, however, it came as a challenge for me, even though I was already in my second year of medical school at the time. I've often wondered why the caring did not come as naturally for me; I had always loved my gran. She loved me so much and was very proud of all my achievements. I will always regret that she died before I could buy her leopard print clothes, perfumes, and shower her with money. I think I show love by giving things, and that may not always be the best way to care as people tend to forget whatever you have done for them. This further decreases the need for money in relationships because once these resources are no longer needed, you also cease to be needed.

My mother was beautiful. She loved dancing and listening to music. I would watch her dance from an early age and wonder if I would ever be as cool as she was. Music was a huge part of our lives. We listened to Lionel Richie, Diana Ross, Marvin Gaye, Miriam Makeba, Caiphus Semenya, Michael Jackson, Otis Redding, The O'Jays—the list was endless. This was a routine weekend occurrence. My grandmother would often be dyeing clothes. If she was going to wear a purple dress the following day, she would ensure that even her underwear would be dyed purple the day before. Purple was one of her favourite colours.

This was all a prelude to my birth, how I came to be and what household the gods felt was befitting me. These were my people. I loved and will love every one of them forever.

I am fortunate enough to be a grown-up that still remembers her childhood as if it happened yesterday. I was born in an NU7 clinic in a township called Mdantsane as mentioned above to a 17-year-old mother who was a child herself on 7 June 1981 at exactly 7:00 p.m. on a very frosty winter night. My mother says it was a very long and painful delivery which was made worse by the other people who were also screaming because they were also in labour. She would always talk in detail about a makoti (young married woman) who started barking like a dog and my mother, in between both their contractions, asked her if it made the pain better. The makoti told her it worked and so when a contraction arrived, my mother also started barking. She cannot remember clearly if it helped but at least at 7:00 p.m., her pain ended because I arrived. Sadly, I was not bearing any gifts but was very hungry. She was still in high school with great aspirations for her future before this unfortunate event happened to her. She then changed from science and biology to history and geography. Did I mention the 'gap year' she had to take to mother me and breastfeed me? A child mothering another child while her mother and oldest sister, my aunt Sindiswa, had to work to provide for all of us.

They provided clothes, food, and an incredibly beautiful life, especially if you were oblivious to living conditions in the rest of the world. This was heaven. We were children and could have been poor by the world's standards, but we were kings because we had it all, and if we didn't, we simply stole it. Our thieving adventures were always about food. The things that belonged to my granny were not for us, but we made them for us. We knew that she was too old to beat us every day and that knowledge made us royalty. We had Arts and Crafts at school but there were no classes to teach us how to make these things. We needed to ensure that we had something for the teacher to mark before the school term ended. I stole anything that was knitted. I just needed the mark, and the teacher could tell that I could not have made such an elaborate scarf, but I would get my mark and go on my merry way. It remains a mystery to me why we had this subject if there were no resources to bring it to fruition. Instead, we had to resort to stealing valuable things from our families, only to lose them by the lunch break.

MY MOTHER AND HER LOVER

"What the heart has once owned and had,
it shall never lose."
—Henry Ward Beecher

The only mistake my mother made was to give in to an infatuation that drove her insane. My father was good looking, charming, and light in complexion (it seems to have been a determining factor in choosing him). He was everything a travelling stranger from Port Elizabeth could ever be. He was perfect, mysterious, and intriguing, unlike the local boys. He had come to visit his 'boxer friends' which made him cool and led to my young and naïve mother falling for him. Mdantsane is still viewed as the Mecca of boxing and this spotlight began when Nkosana 'Happyboy' Mgxaji defeated a Durban fighter, Moses Mthembu, in the Sisa Dukashe stadium on 2 September 1972. Mgxaji went on to win the South African Junior Lightweight title in 1973. Professor Njabulo Ndebele, in his book *Behind sweaty windows,* talks about boxing being the core element of the Mdantsane township. Indeed, many national and international boxers came from Mdantsane. He cited that boxing was a street sport in Mdantsane and continues to be part of our culture and form of entertainment.

I don't know how much sex education both my parents had received up to that time, but she had intercourse at the age of sixteen for the first time with my father and I was made and completed. In a journal article by Carol E. Kaufman[5] on 'Contraceptive use in South Africa under Apartheid', she explains in excruciating detail how the segregation of Africans further worsened the accessibility of contraception to black people after the white minority government brought this program forward in 1974. This became another tool of oppression

Share of females aged 14-19 years who were pregnant in South Africa in 2018 and 2019, by age

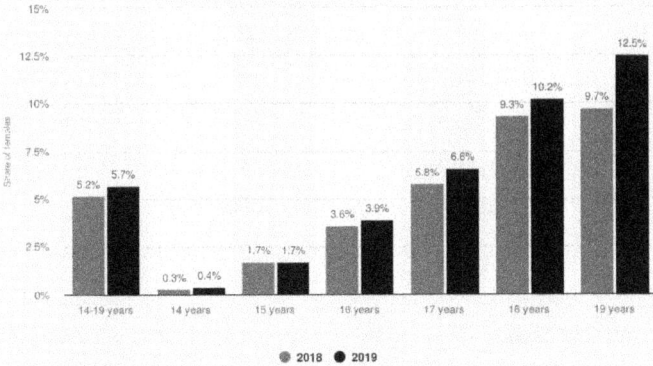

Share of females aged 14-19 years who were pregnant in South Africa in 2018 and 2019, by age from statista.com

as something as basic as contraception became inaccessible to the homelands. Many models were attributed to the problems of the seemingly great program. What was most relevant was the underestimation of how many black people would have wanted this method of birth control, considering that the black population had already reached 75% at that time. In Kaufman's words, "Patterns of contraceptive use among black women in South Africa, as in other parts of the developing world, probably were associated with education, wealth, and urban or rural residence. Other factors particularly important to the South

African context were likely to have given special shape to those relationships: Homeland policies, the labour migration system, and the suspicion by blacks of government policies produced a climate of uncertainty in which reproductive decisions were made." The politics around the implementation of this program resulted in confusion. The questions that arose included whether withholding contraception would not make the already large black population even bigger. This was fought and much research has been done to evaluate what went wrong with the program that black people seemed to have wanted to participate in. The statistics from the South African Department of Health (1969-1993) showed that contraceptive use had been estimated at 44% by the black population in the late 1980s.

I weighed 2.5 kg when I was born. I looked so pale and yellow that people thought my mom had been impregnated by a white person. I wish I could remember the first time I met my mother. I have a strong conviction that at the end of my life I will see my whole life before me and will see that face and see her scared smile. I imagine she must have wondered what she would do with me. I thank her often in my prayers for not aborting me. I thank her openly for giving me a chance at life.

A study[6] conducted by Gladys Bathabile Butha and Johannah Sekudu sought to understand the beliefs and meanings attached to abortion and contraceptives. When the all-white 99% male South African parliament passed the Abortion and Sterilization Act (Act No2 of 1975) which made abortion illegal except under special circumstances, it became a crime to seek an abortion. This law made South Africa experience major dilemmas when it came to abortions and unsafe abortions became the order of the day for both young and unmarried women. These injustices were mitigated during the International Conference on Population Development (ICPD) in 1994 where unsafe abortions were ruled against by different countries as a major health concern which increased mortality and morbidity. I can only think the worst if my mother had chosen that path. We could have both lost our lives in a backstreet abortion gone wrong and our family would have had to carry that stigma for the rest of their lives. There are things that the masses choose not to forgive, no matter how prevalent the practices are. These things remain as curses associated with your family when your secret is revealed.

Her magical decision to give birth to me ensured that I felt love, joy, peace, and the adrenaline of stealing peaches from a neighbour's tree. I have felt extreme pleasure, got educated, travelled, had my children, experienced meaningful friendships, and even more sublime relationships with my family, especially with my aunt who lives in Cape Town. She was my best friend growing up and all my good decisions were inspired by her.

I grew to distinguish between spirituality and religion—a lesson I pray my children will learn much earlier than I did. I fell for a million men, had my heart broken a billion times, and read a lot of books in between. This is because my mother never gave up on me then and she would die not ever having given up on me.

I want to emphasise the importance of having good role models. My aunt in Cape Town was a role model and because of the life she lived, I was inspired to follow suit. I, a little girl from Mdantsane visited the suburbs every December holiday and this ritual changed how I viewed myself for the rest of my life. Being at her house showed us the kind of life we had only seen on TV. We ate everything in excess and our aunt would just buy more. She spoilt us with clothes, perfumes, jewellery, and an endless supply of other things. I had hoped to be that kind of aunt. An experience that I remember clearly was when we arrived in Cape Town on yet another visit and had lice all over our hair. She was so mad at our mothers. The following day she sent us to a beautiful salon to have our heads gently massaged and relaxed. Our mothers were chastised over the phone whilst we giggled in the background. In Cape Town, we were her kids and whatever consequences our mothers would bear did not involve us. There were too many sweets, chips, chocolates to eat than there was time to worry about anyone else.

Since my father was a visitor in Mdantsane, he was not present in our lives. His absence confused me when I watched some of my friends who had fathers, even Nombuyiselo and Songezo (my cousins) had fathers. I imagine that he wished, towards the end of his life, that he had been more present in our lives. Given that he died at the age of twenty-four, I doubt he had enough time to introspect and potentially correct his ways. I don't remember his face. I would have passed him by if I were to see him in a shopping mall. I am told that he came to pay money for damages, which is customary if you had impregnated a woman who was not your wife. He also brought me clothes. Since he was from Port Elizabeth he eventually impregnated someone else, and another the year after that. He must have informed my mother of these additional children and that deeply saddened her as she concluded that she now had a fatherless child. My mother was young, and this must have devastated and traumatised her. I imagine she must have wondered how she was going to tell me this truth in the future.

She repeated the story often, and even though many years had passed, she conveyed it with so much hurt that I could feel it in my heart and see it in her eyes. It was the hurt that you can only experience if you have loved someone deeply enough. I wish that they had spoken about the issues they faced in mortality however enormous they seemed. I hope that in heaven, as heavenly beings, they are at peace. I hope that they are gentle, tender, and merciful towards each other. I hope they are friends and continue to be proud of me. I wish for them to follow my children everywhere they go and, as co-creators with God, make their paths straight. They are my parents and I love them both.

I have no idea how I can explain how I could love a father I had never known. I know that he is my other half and feeling anything different towards him is an act of self-hate. I understand, however, that children and adults have suffered and continue to suffer abuse at the hands of their fathers or even mothers. I pray with you and pray that healing comes in the morning.

With both my parents dead, the issue of immortality rests upon my shoulders. I need to leave something behind—be it a legacy for my children, a tree, a set of values, principles, and whatever inspires goodness, mercy, and justice. I recently came across work that focuses on genetics. I carry half of my genes from my mother and half from my father. My children carry half of my genes and if they too, have children, this biological phenomenon carries on forever. This is merely hoping that who we are lives on, in whatever capacity.

My mother never stopped loving my father. Whether she was mad at him for abandoning us and relinquishing his duty to us or was reciting a dream she had about him, it was always evident that she still loved him, despite the anger. This reminds me of Yves Saint-Laurent and Pierre Bergé. They were divorced but as Bergé put it in his eulogy to Saint-Laurent, the love never died. Admiration of him never faded. Saint-Laurent's profound mental challenges never phased Bergé, never made him love him any less or gave him a reason to leave, to disappear, or to abandon him. I watch him often on YouTube as he greeted people who had come to mourn with him at Yves Saint-Laurent's funeral, he looked fractured and heartbroken. This made me realise that some people love each other forever.

MY CHILDHOOD

"Do not look sad. We shall meet soon again." "Please, Aslan,"
said Lucy, "what do you call soon?" "I call all times soon," said
Aslan; and instantly he was vanished away.
—C. S. Lewis, The Chronicles of Narnia

It is very difficult to find the right words to describe my childhood. It was magical, mystical, and beautiful. Albert Einstein once commented, "Play is the highest form of research" and I agree as my study has found similar conclusions: play provided us with the kind of childhood that our children lack—no technological gadgets, pure-play, and wonder. The only impediment to childhood is how soon it ends. Patrick Rothfuss[7] states, "When we are children we seldom think of the future. This innocence leaves us free to enjoy ourselves as few adults can. The day we fret about the future is the day we leave our childhood behind."

The only magic I can compare my childhood to would be the magic Peter, Susan, Edmund, and Lucy felt when they met Aslan for the first time. I can imagine the feeling of wonder Lucy must have felt as she was not only the first to find the wardrobe, but also the first to see Aslan in the Chronicles of Narnia by C. S. Lewis. Living in a township means you get to have a multitude of friends and get to create your own Narnia. Everything is exactly as you project and will it in your mind—a brick can be a car, period. Friends become your life, except when you are still breastfeeding like I was. I breastfed until I was almost seven years old. Nothing was more serene, more soothing than my mother's breast.

Even as a 40-year-old I can still taste the peace that being held by my mother offered me. It made me feel invincible and loved. As young as I was, I knew my mother loved me. Kids younger than me had long stopped breastfeeding but not me, I only stopped when I was ready to. I still struggle to comprehend how my mother continued breastfeeding for as long as she did.

She must have had friends, boyfriends, and a life outside of me, just like I had a life outside of her.

The love my mother showed me from my birth to her death has been unparalleled. She taught me everything I would need to know for school and did homework with me till I was in standard eight. During those times there was a numbering system given to students in a particular class, I was always number one. This level of apparent genius under the then newly formed Education and Training Act of 1979, which had replaced the notorious Bantu education which had failed black people dismally, gave me some popularity as people needed to copy homework and a lot of other things. I also made a business out of it—times were tough, and I wanted to buy chocolates and russians.

ALLIES

"A life that touches others goes on forever."
— Unknown

A year after I was born, my aunt Phumeza gave birth to a daughter, Nombuyiselo on 17 October 1982. A year thereafter my eldest aunt Sindiswa gave birth to a son, Songezo on 12 March 1983. These two people would be my allies for life. We played, fought, laughed, and cried together. Our home had a big yard, most of the homes had big yards, but the home itself was tiny. All the erf sizes were 300 m². The bigger room belonged to my grandmother. My uncle Vusumzi slept in the lounge and the rest of the family slept in the smaller bedroom. All our friends must have had the same setup. We loved our home. It always had different wallpapers that my grandmother adored. To this day, I have not met someone as stylish and eccentric as my grandmother. You could smell her perfume from the gate, the reason I struggle to use it is that those pungent smells ruined perfume for me forever. She would allow us to sleep on her bedroom floor and she would tell us folklore stories. Those remain the best moments and memories of my life. She loved us. Our mothers were young and sometimes prone to not being around as often, so our grandmother took care of us and never complained about it.

We were exceptionally naughty children, especially Songezo and me. We loved stealing our granny's cokes and replacing them with water. There were three of us and if we all said it was not us, then it was not us. We were denying something every day. Only Nombuyiselo was telling the truth, but we made sure to not do things in front of her. Nombuyiselo and I collaborated to make Songezo our guinea pig. We would steal a hair crème relaxer and tell him that he would look like Michael Jackson. He believed us but by the time we washed it off, all his hair was gone because we had no idea how long it was supposed to be on his hair. Despite this, we also managed to save his life numerous times. He believed that he could swim and would dive into a swimming pool whenever we were on holiday visiting our aunt in Cape Town. Nombuyiselo and I would devise strategies to save him because we also could not swim. We threw everything inside the pool to try and fish him out. Instead of learning from this, he would do the same thing the following day.

Nombuyiselo was more graceful. She was quiet and when people asked her why she was not talking she simply answered that I spoke enough for the two of us. She was smart. She could save money and buy clothes, thus making everyone look at how irresponsible I was since I had no clothes, but debt related to vetkoeks and russians. I was a kid and buying myself clothes instead of KitKat, Bar-One, and chicken feet had never crossed my mind. She bailed me out of my food debts more times than I can remember and each time she would make me promise her that I would stop buying things on credit. Even after this, she continued to sacrifice her lunch money to bail me out. It was as if she knew that we were not going to grow old together. It was as if she knew she would be leaving this earth the year we were to start matric.

She was involved in a car accident and died. The year 1998 was the most painful year of my life as she died in January before school started. I had not yet developed any coping mechanisms to help me deal with my loss. Unfortunately, my family also did not know how to help me in this grief as they were also grieving and looking for answers to alleviate the pain.

She was gone yet she was a child. Children were not thought to die, especially children who were not sick. She was never going to have a blossoming career with all her genius. She would never get married to the love of her life or have children to spoil and raise with lots of discipline. She died with all the wisdom she had tried to impart to me for many years. We had both converted to the Mormon church with the blessings of our parents in our early teens, and now even going to the church was depressing. She was my twin and my best friend. A huge part of me was buried in the ground alongside her.

The very fabric of my life had changed, and it would take many years before I could laugh again and not feel like I was betraying her by moving on. I wish I had understood impermanence at that stage. As Jack Field puts it, "Like a sandcastle, all is temporary. Build it, tend it, enjoy it. And when the time comes, let it go." I have never really been able to let go of Nombuyiselo and her memory. Her death still gnaws at me like there is something that I could have done differently. I will always remember her selflessness, her laugh, her huge hair, and the way she could explain things to me without confusing me. I will always miss her amazing range of expressions, the child-like wonder in her eyes, her ferocity in chasing her dreams, her serene eagerness to follow God's commandments, her quiet content-sensitive nature, her tranquillity, and her fascination with science.

She challenged me endlessly and kept trying new things, even without me. She did karate and had an entire life with her karate friends. I wished I could join but the hours of commitment seemed too much for me and I was not as interested as she was. Our last year together was tumultuous and quickly ended like a bolt of lightning. She had reconnected with her father's family and visited them every weekend and holiday, which meant less time spent with me. In a recent conversation with my aunt, she assured me that this was not a rejection but an extension of her growth as an individual. This is where she lost her life alongside her father's sister who was a mayor at the time and who was the driver of the car that caused the fatal crash. I went to visit her as she lay dying in a hospital in George, so far from home. But I was too late. By the time I arrived, she was already gone.

She had tried desperately to wait for me, but I had to start in Cape Town so that I could travel with my aunt and her family. In the metal slab where they had put her lifeless body, she looked so alive; in fact, she had never looked more alive. She had two fractured femurs and so her face still looked perfect and her long big hair was still intact. I shook her and screamed and begged her to wake up. I knew she would wake up. This was me who had arrived, and she would recognise my voice. We had plans for the rest of our lives so, why would she not wake up? I spent what felt like eternities waking her up until I realised that she was not waking up.

We die in bits and pieces. She had already reached her molecular death, then her sub-atomic death. She had reached a point of no return. I will never forget the stench of death in that cold room. The family is still very prominent in South Africa and now, as a grown-up, I can understand the fascination that she was drawn to—a world that was not her own. A perfect world from the outside that had all the trimmings of a perfect life— ministerial houses, frequent phone calls, take-out foods, endless movie marathons, and overnight cousins that seemed to have accepted and loved her. I will always remember them as the place where I lost her forever. I will remain forever robbed. They had become her life in those last months, yet they disappeared as quickly as they had arrived.

From the day she died something happened that I had never expected would last for as long as it did. She visited me every night in my dreams, and it would always be the same. We would be children again, racing each other, climbing trees together, and stealing peaches with our friends. We were living an entire day every night. Let me give you a snippet of some of the games we would play[8] we would play:

- Three toti—an active game played using a ball and three cans placed like a pyramid. The aim of the game is to hit the three cans.
- Unopey'ntana—a game that gave old pantihose a new purpose. There would be two people on each end, with the pantihose string placed around their bodies to complete various levels of the game.
- Unocheyi—played in a drawn-out square about 4 by 2.
- Upuca—a game played on the ground with small stones. A circle is drawn which marks the boundary in which the stones should be placed. A bigger stone is thrown in the air whilst the player drags the other stones out of the circle. The player then throws the bigger stone in the air again and pushes the rest of the stones back into the circle, leaving a few stones out, depending on the level they are on. The aim of this game is for the player to collect the right number of stones

for the level they are on, without dropping the bigger stone.

I grew to look forward to the nights because she would come back to me without fail. We had different adventures every night and sometimes, we went to places we had never visited before.

I grew up and the dreams never ceased. I went to university and got married and the dreams were always with me. I never shared this with anyone because I was scared nobody would believe me or worse people, especially my mother's family, would think I am crazy, like my father. My mother had spoken about my father's fractured mind towards the end of his life.

I was experiencing living with my beloved cousin every day and was also worried that sharing it with her mom (aunt Phumeza) could make her even sadder as she was now a shadow of her former self and would continue to be for the rest of her life. Between the guilt over aunt Phumeza's possible reaction and my shame at being judged or worse being made to be like my dad, it seemed to suffice to keep this life to myself. The thing that confused me about this experience was that Nombuyiselo stayed the same age, or we were even younger in the dreams. She never grew old although I was growing old. In my late twenties, she left me, not to say she does not come now and again, but her visits became less frequent.

She gave me a chance to concentrate on my life and leave the past behind. I will always be grateful to her for staying with me long after she was physically gone from this world.

This will always be a testament that love never dies, even if we are on different sides of the veil. This knowledge has brought so much meaning to my life and makes me sure that I will never leave my children, even if a tiny veil separates us. This meaning has brought so much comfort and joy, that even as I grieve my beautiful mother, I know that she is not too far from me. I will always be grateful that I met my beloved cousin, and that I was able to meet first-hand someone as selfless, gracious, kind, beautiful, self-sacrificing, smart, and magical as her. She remains my protector and my provider. All the challenges that I have faced since she left have been for my good and to give me the experience to decide what kind of mother I wanted to be. I practise conscience parenting and I am falling in love with the adult person and mother I am becoming.

I would not be doing her the justice she deserves if I did not end her chapter on a note about debt. If I had learnt from her example, I could have prevented the embarrassment faced as my vehicle was repossessed when I was a young intern. My car was taken whilst I was with my son who kept asking where that man was taking the car. This little secret was so damning, and I wished with every fibre of my being that no one would ever hear of it. You can learn from a youthful age to be self-sufficient and save to prevent yourself from going through such embarrassing situations. I implore you to know that your financial soberness is your responsibility and like resilience, one can learn it over time. It all starts with small decisions like saying no to financial products that are not needed, or expensive luxuries whose time has not yet arrived.

CHAPTER 2:
THE FIRST MARRIAGE

*"If only. Those must be the two saddest words
in the world."*

—Mercedes Lackey

It does not matter how much time I spend on this a day, but the truth is that some portion of my day is dedicated to this—the end of my marriage. I go back so many times and revisit what I could have done differently or not done at all. Sometimes it is not the end of the marriage, it is a memory, not a bad memory. I could be passing a place we frequented or could hear a song that my mind associated with my husband, the list of the triggers is endless such as seeing him fetch his children for their two weekends a month.

As a chess player, it would be easy to identify triggers, there are only sixty-four squares and going back is easy. I am an offensive player; my strategy is always scaring my opponent by making big moves from the onset. However, in chess, unlike life, you can see exactly where you became cocky and open your board to a merciless opponent who was patient enough to destroy, but then again, this is a game. The year was 2007 when I met the man who was to become my husband. I was a medical intern in the Pietermaritzburg Complex. It was a gruelling two-year internship filled with many sleepless nights, financial restraints, a pornography addiction that developed in university (medical school to be precise), and a failing marriage, amongst other challenges.

A failing marriage? How is that possible if I am still describing meeting my husband? Well, I was married when I met this husband. The oddest thing is that my pornography addiction, which had been explained to both the men I was to marry, became very different whilst married. Both used that information to torture and abuse me as if it was information that had been kept from them, an utter lie. I have continued to struggle with the shame that this addiction has brought into my life and its blessing of showing me the people that were in my life for real reasons.

What led me to develop a pornography addiction? I think it had to do with having sexual restraints when biologically and physiologically you are at your sexual peak. The agonies, highs and ecstasies of that thrill were addictive even though the extent of it was not a daily or weekly occurrence. A more aggressive addiction would have made me less functional, and the medical school needed my highest emotional, mental, and intellectual functioning. I would stop many times, but the beckoning of this worsening tide was beyond me, and the longing and desire would take me back to the version of myself I despised.

I was so disillusioned by the many circumstances around me. The stand to try and be morally correct and virtuous was indeed taxing. I was a Mormon, yet I still had urges like other people my age. This is not something that I could run away from. I still watch porn but very rarely. I am a middle-aged woman now and its appeal is no longer as huge as it once was. I don't wish it for my children though. The amount of guilt and shame spent on it is a true waste of time. The humiliation you receive from the people you trusted with your secret is not worth it. I was not the only young woman who had this interest in exploring pornography; it must have come with independence as well. I remember a night when two of my girlfriends and I decided to go to one of the shops that sell these DVDs and we bought three. It remains one of our best memories. We went back to our residence and whilst giggling as if we were on a high, we watched the forbidden acts. The funniest thing was that they left one by one to meet with their boyfriends and since I was boyfriend-less I stayed and wondered what to do with the key. I was left alone in one of my friend's rooms and it was hilarious.

We have spoken about that night many times and unfortunately, one of them succumbed to COVID-19. Now that memory has two people that keep it and one day there will be only one of us who will have no one to share it with. It will be her story to smile and remember on her own.

I remember receiving a couple of articles from my second husband who claimed that pornography was cheating. He revealed all of this at the end of the marriage, even though he was the one that decided to marry someone who watched porn and had not promised to stop watching it. We had never even seen a therapist for the problem that he married me with, yet he claimed we saw counsellors over this problem. Hopefully, he has proof of the so-called interventions. My husband had a choice to not associate with someone who watches porn or worse even marry them.

My next problem with my second husband became cooking. I had declared that I could not cook even before the marriage and in the three years, we lived together before getting married. I worked long hours to maintain our lifestyle and even though I studied Dietetics, I still did not enjoy cooking. This was not a problem, instead, it was a joke in our relationship. However, it became a huge problem when he became a chartered accountant after he had received the gifts that he had come for. These gifts included expensive clothes that he now wore, expensive suits including Hilton Weiner and Polo. He got dental implants (tooth roots made of titanium) that provided perfect teeth instead of the crooked ones that he had when we met. I paid a maxillofacial around R50 000 for that and his mistresses received instant perfect smiles, a red sports car, et cetera. I had to compromise by cooking two different roasts every Sunday. I started wearing weaves now and then but despite this, my marriage was still crumbling.

We could have avoided so much pain had he been true to himself and not used pornography as a bargaining chip in the middle of a war. We would never have gotten married because I had never committed to stopping. This was the same as my first husband who kept telling me that the pornography people had come by the house looking for me. As if people from Shoprite come to your home and tell you that you have not bought the milk you buy daily. Both my husbands never paid lobola for me. This further lowered my self-esteem and made me feel worthless. The Church of Jesus Christ of Latter-day Saints (LDS), sometimes referred to as the Mormon Church, does not support this cultural practice of lobola. Even though it made me a joke at home, I was listening to the prophet, seers and revelators, and that gave me some comfort. Also, with my feelings of unworthiness follow-ing my many experiences and established pornography addiction, it felt as though I was paying some debt. I felt that I would finally be accepted and seen as worthy, spiritual, and be married in the temple like all the righteous people.

MY FIRST HUSBAND

"Your mind marries many ideas. You marry beliefs, opinions, dogmas, concepts, theories, creeds; whatever you mentally and emotionally unite with in your mind, that's a marriage. Psychologically, your marriage partner is your idea, your concept of yourself, your estimate of yourself, your blueprint."
— **Dr Joseph Murphy,**
The Power of Your Subconscious Mind

When I read the quote by Dr Joseph about who you marry I was taken aback. My first husband was my blueprint; my mind married the idea of him, yet I knew nothing about him. I just really wanted to do right by the Mormon standards, and this would make my fascination with pornography go away, and it did for the longest time. It was like killing two birds with one stone. I had never been more wrong in my then twenty-three years of life. I read the words at the beginning of the chapter and breakdown from my desperation and despair. I had made up my mind about this decision and I cry for the innocence of that person I used to be who got married for all the wrong reasons, to the wrong person. I married a man and had no idea what our future would be like.

There was no sense of futurity from the first day but promises of greatness to come. I still remember saying, "I do" on our wedding day and there have never been other words I have uttered in my life that were more bewildered and muddled.

I met my first husband as a teenager at church in Mdantsane. He was so handsome, with impeccable hair, dark skin, short (the only imperfect thing about him). Everything of his had been put in the right place by the Almighty. There were plenty of us who wanted to date him. He was new to the Mormon Church which I had been a member of since I was fourteen or fifteen years old. He made it clear to us that he was dating a lady who was not a member of the Mormon church. This was a huge disappointment for my teenage self, and my fragile ego was shattered. I was a committed Mormon and believed in the Eternal dream. Being a teenager though provides some protection because there are friends, church, and school to worry about. I went back to worrying about the important things that seriously needed my attention.

After matric, I moved to Pietermaritzburg where I studied for my first degree, a Bachelor of Science in Dietetics. I remember how my mother quizzed me about the choice of degree and I just wanted to study something that would assist me to become a better wife in the future. I explained this confidently to my mother, of all people. I went on to explain that I would be able to cook for my future husband and future children. She looked at me with a mischievous smile that reminded me that I did not have a date for my matric dance, which brought on the realisation that the husband was going to take his own sweet time to arrive.

If there is one thing you are taught as a Mormon is this: marriage will make you happy and even bring you exaltation, a concept that I will touch on in the next chapter. Marriage will cure whatever insecurities your childhood may have presented and as the perfectionist that I was, I knew I was going to marry "a returned missionary" (a young man who had served the Lord for two years away from their home and brought the truth of the only true church to the rest of the world). This practice continues to this day where boys and sometimes girls were even taken to places that had the deadliest diseases like Ebola. I believed that it would cure me and give me the self-esteem I craved and the direction that I needed.

I had completely forgotten that even the members of the church were human and that even these so-called truths they were teaching me were not known to them as a certainty. I have since learnt that only raw human experience can bring you realities that you know for sure. I know for sure that there is no religion or any well-meaning sect that can bring me Eternal life or even a shred of peace, or even something as intangible as happiness. Only I can bring that to myself. I experience a fullness of life through living my best life and being my best self each day that I live. Ensuring that I am in touch with even the most subtle subatomic levels of myself is where I thrive and become the best me.

I thought my stand would guarantee me a place near Jesus at the end of my life. I will never regret the years spent holding on to those beliefs. They gave me a moral code, a compass, yes the compass was Jesus, but I was saved from many things that girls from the townships are weak to succumb to, drugs, alcohol, sex and in the end, HIV infection. I lost many dear friends to HIV/AIDS and when I think about it now, we were children when some of us died. They died too soon and the teachings about abstinence, be faithful and condoms were not enough. Maybe people needed to die before we could realise that HIV/AIDS kills. I tell this story from the perspective of the teenager that I was, not as the adult clinician I am now. Indeed, much research and labouring has been done in the field such that we have innovative treatment that is aimed at decreasing the morbidity and mortality associated with HIV infection.

When I was younger, even the politicians were divided in terms of the causal aspects of either HIV or

AIDS. It continued to be a conundrum of confusion for many years as opportunistic infections like pulmonary tuberculosis (PTB) took their toll on our untreated population. Some organisations decided to smuggle drugs across different countries as they watched people dying. They risked their lives trying to save lives whilst the government took their time to decide on what needed to be done. I am sure many books have been written on these atrocious and fascinating times. They will always form a part of my history.

I continued having some correspondence with him through the new cell phones. My mother had bought me one and it was a sublime present. He liked me when I was older and announced that his relationship had ended. He then went on to serve as a missionary of The Church of Jesus Christ of Latter-Day Saints for an entire two years. He returned 'with honour' as they termed those who had returned without having done any immoral acts or whatever was deemed unworthy during their time away. He spread the message of the gospel of Jesus Christ and brought many souls unto Christ. The message of the Mormon church is peculiar, and its history is filled with many holes.

When I was in my fourth year of medical school, the good-looking guy and I became a thing in the Summer of 2004. He was still good-looking and spiritually right, so when he wanted us to get married I was over the moon. I did not see his plans for his future, but it seemed as though things were going to miraculously fall into place. We got married in late March 2005 after three months of dating.

There was an Institute Summer class on Eternal marriage taught by a male member of the church that I admired. He mentioned that there was no such thing as soul mates. All it took to marry someone was to ensure that their values aligned with yours and God. If we were both great members of the church, our marriage would stand the test of time.

We had not kissed nor had sex before our wedding day and were blessed with a honeymoon baby. My first baby, a beautiful baby boy born with skin as yellow as his mother that the doctors thought he had jaundice. He is the true love of my life because when this marriage ended, it was just me and him. I am yet to love another human being with as much strength.

I will elaborate on the Mormon doctrine of marrying in a temple and what goes on there, suffice to write for now that I went to the temple once, when I was marrying this man. Most Mormons do the pilgrimage to the temple at least twice a year if they live far from Johannesburg. I went once, and that was more than enough. Our marriage was short-lived, by the time my son turned two we were already separated.

My dream of meeting my future husband was limited to teachings in the church on soul mates. I was never going to meet him in some coffee shop, or reaching out for a book in a bookstore, or just on a lazy day by the beach. The number of divorces in my age group certainly disputed that fact. You hear a new story of a couple separating more times than the people you know outside the church. Little did my most honoured and admired advisor know that his advice brought the beginning of hell itself for I had followed his idea precisely. My son does not remember meeting his father nor the time we spent as a family when he was younger. That protects him, somehow. Remembering may have put a strain on his young mind yet with everything we know about the brain now, we know it does not forget. We know that traumas suffered as far back as in utero are significant and can alter the course of a life. We, however, live in a state of never-ending hopefulness.

I recently had a casual conversation with my son and asked him what the absence of a father meant to him. How did he feel about only finding out about him at age eleven? He said that as long as his father could not provide proof to show that he had done everything possible to fight to see him—a letter from the social workers or family advocates—he continues to concentrate on the parent that has been with him from day one. He focuses on the parent who is always there, the one who has given him opportunities and cheered him along in his endeavours. I spoke to him briefly about the R700 maintenance that his father pays possibly five times a year. My son begged me to leave him alone with talks of this money. We are not pursuing him, and I am trying to save for my son's university fees.

Even a teenager could see through the folklore stories he was told by an absent father about a mother who he knows had sacrificed everything for him. My son promises me though that when he is ready, he will try to reach out to him and maybe make peace with him. He is not sure when that will be but promises it will happen one day.

CHAPTER 3:

THE MORMON CHURCH

MEMBERSHIP/ PRISON NUMBER
05400487672

"We thank thee oh God for a prophet."
—**Hymn from the LDS church**

I received my Patriarchal Blessing when I was sixteen years old, and it was recorded as it was said to me. The blessing is given by a Patriarch which is a highly spiritual member of the church that is closer to God than most other members of the church. Hands are laid on your confused but grateful head and mind. The blessing is usually broken into three parts: the life before you came on earth, your life on earth, and your life after you have left this world. Imagine that kind of information overload for a teenager. I was promised a husband who would love me and take me to the temple. I was also promised children and that my faithfulness would guarantee that I met the Saviour at his coming. The main theme of the entire blessing is your faithfulness. I wanted to receive these blessings and promised myself to be faithful no matter what.

My cousin was still alive when we received the blessings. We were taught to never share our blessings with anyone. It was our little secret. I was confused when I found my cousin's blessing after she had died which read the same as mine, word for word. She had also been promised this husband and children and things related to life on earth. Little is mentioned about school and success, even though we were from a township. Part of our future would surely have had to include university so that we could have a better future and could contribute to making our family life better. It seemed odd, but as a teenager, so many things are on your mind that you dismiss this discrepancy. Why was it the same blessing? Were we not two separate individuals? She died, but she would also have had all these earthly blessings. I could not ask anyone since a Patriarchal Blessing is secretive so, I had to be the gatekeeper of our blessings and secrets.

Patriarchal Blessing

Date of blessing (day, month, year)		Patriarchal blessing number
9 July 1997		138

Recipient (first, middle, surname)
Zikhona Angelique Hlalempini.

Birthdate (day, month, year)	Birthplace (city, county, state/nation)
7 June 1981	Mdantsane, East London, South Africa.

Father's name (first, middle, surname)	Mother's maiden name (first, middle, surname)
Zuzile Sibali.	Ncumisa Hlalempini.

Patriarch	Stake
Johannes P Brummer	Johannesburg, South Africa

Dear Sister Zikhona Angelique Hlalempini, as a humble servant of our Lord Jesus Christ, and of our Heavenly Father, by the authority of the Holy Melchezidek Priesthood, in the Office of Patriarch, in the Church of Jesus Christ of Latter-Day Saints, I lay my hands upon your head, to give you your Patriarchal blessing. I pray our Heavenly Father will bless me, and use me as His Instrument and Voice, to give you your blessing concerning your life's sojourn here on Earth, and throughout all eternity.

Dear Sister, you are a choice daughter of our Heavenly Father, born of goodly parents, and blessed by our Father in Heaven, and our Saviour the Lord Jesus Christ. You were blessed in the Council of Spirits, in the pre-earth life, held to be born in these the latter days, in the Dispensation of the Fullness of Times. You loved the Saviour, and sided with Him in the Plan of Salvation, when our Father presented the Plan to all His Spirit children.

You loved the Redeemer and Father in Heaven, when the beauty of the gospel, of the Lord came into your life here on Earth, you recognised the truth, and the love you had for it, this lightened your heart and mind, you embraced the truth, and accepted your Lord Jesus Christ again with a great love, and took upon you His Holy and Sacred name, and entered the waters of Baptism, and received the great blessing of the Gift of the Holy Ghost. You truly again became, a loving supporter and daughter, of your Lord and Master, Jesus The Christ, and of our Heavenly Father.

Dear Sister, you are greatly blessed with the Spirit, and the love for your Redeemer the Lord Jesus Christ. As you have read the scriptures, and have felt of the Spirit of the Lord, the Holy Spirit witnessed to you, in your inner most soul, of the truthfulness of the gospel, and that Jesus is the Christ, the Son of the Living God our Father in Heaven. You love them, and have a knowledge of the Spirit They love you, and you are Their daughter.

For the great love you have, for your Creator, the Lord your God has blessed you, as a daughter of Abraham, blessed into the Household of Israel, of the lineage of Ephraim, the son of Joseph, and blessed with all the blessings the Great Jehovah, blessed these great Patriarchal fathers, the Prophets and their families of old, and all the blessings they received from the Lord, are sealed upon your head.

I bless you on this day, as you are busy with your studies, you are in your youth, preparing your life's education, to achieve in your schooling, for your mind and intellect to be opened, and enlightened, as you learn of the teachings of life, of things upon the Earth above and below, of that which is important in life, to help you in your career of your choice, and have your mind enlightened, to retain the knowledge, of the teachings you receive, to be a blessing and help to you, as this will prove a help to many of our Father's children.

In you are many talents, many of them are latent, which you have not yet discovered. I bless you as you prayerfully ask for an answer from the Lord your God, and apply the true teachings of the gospel, prayerfully seek The Father for the answer to your talents, the Lord will open your heart, your mind and understanding, and these talents that are within you, will become alive. You will be blessed to be a great blessing, in the Hands of your Redeemer, to your family and our Father's children.

Dear Sister, our Heavenly Father has blessed, and well-loved you from above, and blessed this day, as you study the Holy Scriptures of the Lord, read and prayerfully ponder upon them. The Lord will open your mind and intellect to receive great understanding of light and truth, of the beautiful doctrines of the Kingdom, and the teachings of the Lord, the mysteries of the Kingdom of God will unfold to you, and you will receive great light and truth.

Your tongue will be loosened, to be a blessing of testimony, to all those whom our Lord will inspire you through the Holy Spirit, to testify and to teach, and to share the beautiful truths of the gospel, you are blessed with this day, to these sacred blessings, of being a witness of your Lord and Saviour Jesus The Christ.

Your body is the Temple of the Lord, His Spirit child, and the Lord's Spirit dwells only in clean and pure bodies. Thus I bless you with the strength, power, the courage and the blessing, to live the Word of Wisdom, a commandment of the Lord, a law of health that will bless your body, and keep it pure and clean, healthy and strong, blessed with marrow in your bones, and strength in your sinews, blessed with great treasures of knowledge, wisdom and powers of resistance, against the evils that will come in your life in these days, for all the plagues, illnesses, sicknesses and diseases that will cover the face of the Earth, in your life time. I bless you with the power to overcome, and the Destroying Angel shall pass you by.

I bless you with a love in your heart, for your parents and loved ones, honour and love them, and receive the blessing of the Spirit of Elijah in your soul, research the records and family history of your loved ones, submit and take them to the House of the Lord, to have the Holy Sacred Ordinances of Salvation done for them. Those who have passed on are in Spirit Prison, they are hearing the gospel of the Lord, and are waiting for the Ordinances to be done for them to enter Paradise, the Kingdom of the Lord, to prepare themselves for the Great Second Coming of our Lord and Saviour Jesus Christ, and as you accomplish this, you will be a saviour on Mount Zion for your loved ones.

Dear Sister, as you walk in faithfulness before the Lord, you are blessed this day, as you prayerfully prepare yourself, and live in righteousness, the Lord will bless you that the day will come, when a righteous Priesthood Holder will come into your life. He will love you, and you will love him. He will take you to the Holy House of the Lord, and bless you to be sealed to him, to receive the blessings of Eternal Life, and Eternal Lives. And receive the blessings of Abraham Isaac, and Jacob, the blessings that your posterity and generations will multiply throughout all eternity. You and your husband will receive the blessings of kingdoms, thrones, principalities and exaltations, with all the blessings our Father can pour out upon you, according to your faithfulness.

I bless you as you walk in faithfulness before the Lord, as you mature in the gospel, you will receive the blessing to be called through the Holy Priesthood of God, to be a leader among the daughters of our Father in Heaven, in His Church and Kingdom, and be a blessing to them, a counsellor in spiritual things, and a blessing of light and truth.

For your faithfulness and love for the Lord, you are blessed to rise in the Morning of the First Resurrection, the Resurrection of the Just, when our Saviour comes in Clouds of Glory, to receive the righteous unto Himself. You and your righteous family, will be called up into the Heavens, to join the righteous Assemblies of our Lord, to rejoice and sing anthems of Glory to our Father and our Saviour, and thank your Saviour and Redeemer for His Great Atoning Sacrifice, and blessed to be presented to the Father, to enter the Rest of the Lord, and receive your eternal blessings and reward.

Be faithful and walk in humility, and love our Father's children, strive to obtain the pure love of Christ in your heart, the blessing you are blessed with now, and to always throughout your life to bring our Father's children unto Christ, and you will be crowned with many blessings, from our Father and our Saviour. These blessings I bless you with, and seal upon you, by the Power of the Holy Priesthood, in the Holy sacred name of our Lord and Saviour, our Redeemer Jesus Christ. Amen.

PATRIARCH.
Johannes P Brummer.

The secret Patriarchal Blessing you have just read is what the Mormon Church uses to have absolute control over you because these blessings are not just for this life but include Eternities. The stage had been set for me, long before the church delivered atrocities in my life. I was so desperate for these blessings that I would try to be the perfect version of myself all the time. Was that even me or just a cloned version of me who wanted Eternal Life and Exaltation?

The church's core message, apart from that of the resurrected Saviour, is to teach about a man whose name is Joseph Smith who died a martyr along with his big brother who followed him and built the church whilst believing his vision. His vision is contained in the Book of Mormon, and it is stated that when Joseph was fourteen, he had a vision that led him to a place where golden plates were deposited. An angel by the name of Moroni, the last character mentioned in the Book of Mormon, gave them to him. These plates were written in the reformed Egyptian language and 116 pages of the translated ones got lost. This is because a man named Martin Harris, who was a scribe during the two months of work on these 116 pages, appeared to be an investor and needed to prove to his family that he did indeed behold such plates and subsequent translation.

The rest of the golden plates were translated, and other scriptures followed such as the Doctrine and

Covenants, additions to the Bible such as the Pearl of Great Price. As you become a member, you are invited to pray over these sacred books and beliefs and are taught other important laws before you are a full member of the church. These laws include the law of chastity (no sex or other sexual experiments before marriage), word of wisdom (eating healthy, exercise, no tea, no coffee, no tobacco, no alcohol). The law of tithing is set out in Malachi 3:8-12. Malachi 3:10 (King James Version) reads, "Bring ye all the tithes into the storehouse, that there may be meat in mine house, and prove me now herewith, saith the Lord of hosts, if I will not open you the windows of heaven, and pour you out a blessing, that there shall not be room enough to receive it." This has always been one of my favourite scriptures, but nothing has ever compared to Samuel, I'm sure a reluctant leader of Israelites who wanted to be their king. The conversation with God where he explains to him that it is not him Samuel, the man, they are rejecting rather God, who should have been their true King.

I thought often about this scripture and as a young girl, it became my moral compass. I prayed that my actions were not in defiance with my Maker, yet I was so young, there would be so many sins ahead of me and that grace was something and continues to be something freely available. I watch my teenage sons and am grateful that they are not growing up under such intense laws and scrutiny and self-loathing because they are not doing or being what they are supposed to be. They are just boys, and they care more about sports than Eternal Life. They are not going gentle into that good night, like Dylan Thomas, they are drinking life to the lees, like Ulysses by Alfred Lord Tennyson.

I believed it all and whether it was the Holy Ghost or all the dances we went to with other youths around our age from nearby branches, I felt I wanted the baptism alongside my dear cousin Nombuyiselo who quickly got into a very serious relationship with a great guy who would later go and serve a mission. It was during this mission that my cousin passed away. He never got to say goodbye to her and that must have been painful.

We were baptised in a swimming pool of a member's house in Bonnie Doon, East London. Many of us were baptised on that day. Our family was also there and seeing them support us in an endeavour that they didn't fully understand with a Bible they did not know, The Book of Mormon, was truly moving. It also never made sense to them that we chose a church that does not even have a building whereas our family Presbyterian church has been standing for decades. We worshipped in a school until we got our building many years later, by then I was already in university. Our family respected our choice, nonetheless.

Another important ideal in the Mormon church is that of the three degrees of glory. The Telestial, Terrestrial, Celestial kingdoms of glory. The LDS church has based these degrees of glory on the glory of the stars mentioned by Apostle Paul in 1 Corinthians 15-41. Telestial is the lowest degree of glory, followed by the Terrestrial glory of the moon. The Celestial is the highest degree of glory. This is where God and Christ are the judges of all. The criteria needed to live with God and Jesus Christ are according to the Doctrine and Covenants 76:50-53.

- Receive and be valiant in the testimony of Jesus Christ.
- Be baptised in the name of Jesus Christ.
- Receive the Gift of the Holy Ghost.
- Be washed and cleansed from all sins.
- Overcome by faith and endure to the end.
- Be sealed by the Holy Spirit of Promise.

Every Mormon wants to be exalted. To be exalted, you must be a sealed husband and wife. Sealing means you get married in the temple for all time and all eternity. I was sealed with my first husband in a Johannesburg temple with my friend present as a witness. Everyone is dressed in white. The set-up was odd, but I was chasing Eternal Life, right? They made us watch different videos that showed Jesus Christ and Heavenly Father on a screen, so if you lived in an era before projectors and televisions you were sadly never going to experience seeing them. This, I think, was the endowment as I had to make a lot of signs that did not make sense to me. For the first time in my life, it felt as though I was in a cult. We were taught to never discuss the things that happened there, but they were weird. We looked at mirrors that went on forever and represented Eternities. Just before the ceremony begins, you are given a new name. I'm sad to report that I forgot my 'true' name the same day it was given to me. It was a Caucasian name and did not resonate with a Xhosa woman like me. Did my Maker not realise that I was Xhosa and that any other name could not represent me? Eternal marriage is what you crave as a teenager because in between your sadness over the martyrdom of Joseph and Hyrum Smith, you just want to continue their vision in the way you live your life. You want their deaths to count for something

Imagine all the explaining I had to do when CNN reported that Joseph Smith had fourteen wives. How I remembered history was that polygamy started with Brigham Young's presidency after Joseph was killed and it was a revelation. When CNN taught me that one of his wives was fourteen years old, I was crushed. The explanations flooded after that and there were even suggestions that there was no intimacy in those marriages, and they were only for sealing purposes. Sins of omission are also as devastating because I never saw the church in the same way again. The worst was when a forger that had forged many so-called lost church documents was revealed. This was huge because the church, which is led by a prophet, had accepted the earlier forgeries to be true.

I was taught that our church was the only true church upon the face of the earth. We were led by prophets, seers and revelators and some information should have been given to us during the time we were being prepared for baptism such as that black men were not given the Priesthood, which is the authority granted to men on earth to act in the way God wants them to and bless their families and also allows them to receive the endowment and sealing ordinance. They received the Priesthood only in 1978 and an essay was published in 2013 explaining that the ban on the Priesthood was more of a racist act than it was a revelation.

All the above and my confusion over the stand the church has established over the LGBTQIA+ community just killed it for me. If your parents are gay you cannot be baptised and can only be baptised when you renounce them and move out of your home at the age of eighteen. I'm not sure where you are supposed to live after that or who would pay for your education after high school. I can imagine what it must be like for those non-baptised children when they are watching their eight-year-old friends getting baptised. I am concerned about those confused conversations of little children and wonder if the people who advise the church are qualified in child psychology and child psychiatry, or whether this is a revelation that will be retracted when its full effects have been revealed. What traumas exist for those children? Will the church bear any responsibility except thanking God for their prophet? I refuse for my children to ever be in the closet or to attend a church that is not wholly equipped with handling such needs.

Their publications over their recommendations on such policies render me speechless as a mother. If that season ever enters my home at any point, we as a family will find a place that will be accommodative for us all. Where same-sex marriages are performed and families can truly be together forever under their own rules with no judgements because sadly, God is not among us, we don't have his address, but we try as best as we can to live purposeful lives.

My faith started dwindling around this period and it would take years before I could realise that this truth no longer worked for me. The saddest thing is that these righteous people had secrets too. Where does the prophet go when he has erred? Are these just meant for mere mortals? Are they gods? They are mortal which is the one thing that distinguished gods like Zeus and mortals.

Three months before my mother and aunt Phumeza died, I felt a strong prompting to tell them something that had happened to me in the LDS church when I was younger. Some people will see this story as a type of resistance, a way to tarnish the reputation of LDS. This is not some grandstand, this is merely the truth, my truth. It is a truth I have decided to share so that no other female teenager would go through the hell I went through in a church. Most of the people that were there are still alive. They can all tell their story if it is different from mine. I was seventeen when I left to study Dietetics in Pietermaritzburg, KwaZulu-Natal (KZN). I met a guy shortly after I turned eighteen. We fell in love and are still in touch to this day. We had such an intense love affair that was hindered by the commitments that I had made when I joined the church. We eventually engaged in coitus as painful as that was for me since I was now breaking the vows I had made, and this was during my last year. When I came home in June I voluntarily told my Bishop about this, and I was put on probation which usually lasts six months and must be accompanied by an intense kind of repentance for that sin. I was very confident when I came out of that meeting but sadly, the six months were going to turn into years—I just didn't know it yet.

I went back to school and slept with him again and when I returned home in December, I voluntarily told my Bishop again about the sexual acts in a room that had just me and him, in an attempt at repentance once again. He decided that my story was beyond saving by himself and appointed a council to deal with me. The bursary that I had received from church was cancelled with immediate effect. I had to tell the administration lady what I had done so that they cancel it immediately. Did I also mention that it did not matter how repentant and sorry I was, I was just going to pay the ultimate price? I was now a sinner, a promiscuous young lady, by their standards. What they could not see at the time were the sins that would be committed by their precious children. Their children got away with so many inappropriate behaviours and I can bet my life that their membership records and files are clean. There are no punishments, no councils, as long as they came back, they were worthy of callings, only to disappoint their parents again. It is baffling how these great spiritual men found it to be so urgent to punish me and when the time came for their children, life continued as usual. Now my private life was not just known by my judges and executors, but by other people in the church as well.

I was a sinner, and no mercy would be shown to me, instead, a recommendation was made that I should stop school and take a couple of years thinking about my sins in a township where I could get into all sorts of trouble because of my age. The saddest part of this entire show was that nobody cared or sensed that I was terribly sorry. This was of no consequence. The sinner was found guilty.

Do you know these same people asked me years later to start doing medicals for their missionaries that were going to serve their two years in the mission field when I became a doctor in private practice? I asked for no financial compensation by choice. I watched the church that had rejected me now require my services. It was pathetic and hypocritical. I did the work for years. It was an intense irony. I was suddenly perfect enough to serve them using the very degree whose bursary had been taken before the first year of medical school. They selectively forgot that the bursary was cancelled when I sinned.

During my hearing, there may have been twelve men, all old, some black and some white. They kept asking me if I had oral sex, or anal sex, or vaginal sex. I did not even meet the criteria in the church manual of 2001 that required me to be at this hearing:

- I was not an endowed member of the church. These members wear special garments that have different markings underneath their clothes and have made special covenants in the temple. They perform work in respect of the dead and they have received special ordinances and did those eerie and supernatural signs and kept watching those videos of God and Jesus Christ—who look identical, by the way.
- I was not married, nor had I slept with a married man whose punishment usually warranted an excommunication.
- I had not had an abortion or miscarriage.

- I had not stolen any money from the church which also warrants an excommunication, depending on your standing in the church.
- I also had not committed any incest or any public demonstrations of opposition against the church.
- I had not committed a murder.
- I had not engaged in any child pornography.

My fate rested on those righteous brothers who gave themselves that right without being guided by any church manual. They did not spare a thought of some of the mental, emotional, and psychological effects that this ordeal would have on me. I was just another black child who they probably forgot about as soon as their 'righteous punishment' was passed on me. They must have gone home to cosy lunches and dinners whilst I had to explain to my mother that the church bursary was gone. It must also be understood that during your time of being recruited into the church, there was not even one discussion on church justice and how it can be carried out on children without their parents present. Instead, we were taught all the fluffy stuff; faith, repentance, and receiving the Holy Ghost. The depths of the repentance processes were never explained to our parents who now had to foot the bill of a child with nightmares every night. Bills that they had not budgeted for on their meagre salaries. My mother was a poor teacher who had to look after three children on her own.

Another interesting note to add is that the same man who had recommended that I stop school, stay at home, and concentrate on my repentance programme became a home teacher in my home with his wife many years later. Home teachers are allocated to each family unit and assist with challenges in the home or most cases share a message from many of the church magazines. He spoke to me about a member of the church I had known since childhood, who had transgressed whilst holding the office of a Bishop and how many years of ex-communication he faced because of the adulterous sin he had committed. I was livid and told him that I too had been deemed unfit and unworthy and I was not the right person to share this gossip with. They ask us to seek repentance and when we do, they show us no mercy or privacy. Is this also contained in the manuals of the church, to gossip about people's sins? This member now works at the temple because he is a god; he can gossip about people's sins and receive no punishment.

I stand here and ask my accusers this question still: where did they find the information that they decided to use on me? Which church manual supported this sexual atrocity that happened to me? Was it a sexual experiment in case some of them had some type of sexual dysfunction to question a young child as they mentally addressed me about such inappropriate things? Did the church order them to sexually abuse me, to sexually abuse my mind?

Do they know that they became the triggers to the mental scourges that I suffer from till now? Do they know that I continue to suffer from post-traumatic stress disorder because of this? Do they know that more than two decades later, I am still on medication for the anxiety and all the effects they had on me? Did they target me because I was not their daughter, or I was black? The church withheld the Priesthood to black men due to reasons of racism. Was I targeted because of my age? Why was I mauled into this encounter without my family or another older female present, since I was indeed young? I had already been asked to tell the bursary lady about my sexual sins, so confidentiality was not an issue here. A person could have been called to support a teenager. Was this a case of patriarchy within the church? Why was I ostracised from my family whereas my family was needed when they wanted to baptise me?

It took hours and as it went on I could feel my brain being grated like the way you grate carrots. It eventually became clear to me that I was a mere mortal, in the company of gods who were now punishing my evil doings just as the Greek and Roman gods who had such power over their mortals. I wondered what more calamities will visit me besides the church bursary being taken. Indeed, the church ceased to be a place of refuge, a place of forgiveness because to be part of this one, only one thing was required of me, that I become perfect.

I was asked to wait outside while they were dealing with my case, which is why I state my prison number at the beginning of this section. Suddenly, I was a case, as they were deciding on the appropriate punishment for a repentant person who just wanted a second chance. I had performed something done by so many people my age. I was called back inside the room and was told that there were two options they had to choose from: excommunication and disfellowshipment. Excommunication would mean that I would no longer be a member of the church. I would have had to be re-baptised when they saw it fit that my repentance was complete. My name and membership would be blotted out. I would still be allowed to attend church but would be like a visitor. They chose disfellowshipment which took away many privileges. I was just a member of the church with minimal participation—no prayers, no callings.

I was instructed to never pray in church even though people would ask me to pray during the different classes that were held in the church. The church, by this time, had three different sessions per service and I had to keep excusing myself and in a way, my story was known by the masses. There was no protection for my personal space or secrets. I had to read scriptures for specified amounts of time, not to ever partake of the sacrament (this is one of the rituals practised every Sunday where you eat the body of Christ and drink of his blood during a sacrament meeting) until my disfellowshipment tenure was over. I was instructed to never see the boy who had broken up with me because of my self-loathing after the act.

This tenure lasted years and my family asked why I didn't leave the church at that point. They had never read about the legend of the thorn bird, that its main goal is to find the sharpest thorn tree and impale its breast without the thought of the impending death to come. I, like the thorn bird, had gone too far and the dream of an Eternal life was already sold to me, and I was prepared to die waiting for that dream, that perfect life. I continued to impale my very soul on something that did not make sense anymore. I believed in this Joseph Smith. I had already come too far to quit.

The sexual nature of the questions without a parent present was appalling. Why did they care if the sex involved oral sex or anal sex? Why was its frequency an issue? Why did I have to explain how sex is done like some sex guru or prostitute? Did they not have any idea that those questions were dirty and inexcusable? It was sex. It didn't make any sense why that had to be explained. I was humiliated for hours answering things that I had already answered. There was even a court type situation where I was told the one lawyer would represent me and the other one represented the church. I never saw how this person represented me.

I had no support system and had no clue what I was going to say at home since the bursary was gone. Luckily, my aunt from Cape Town saved the day and I was able to register for medical school. I then received a full bursary from the Eastern Cape Department of Health that paid for everything. What the men who put me through this terrible ordeal didn't realise was that this little journey of ours would take my entire lifetime to deal with. The low self-esteem, self-doubt, and self-loathing would take years to process. I had these recurring dreams where I was in this boxing ring and fighting this unknown person and the entire church was always there, laughing, giggling, hurling insults at me, and destroying whatever little dignity I had left.

My mother and aunt were angry and wanted answers and did not understand why the church did not ask to see them when they experienced behavioural problems with me. I kept explaining that even though I had never come across a church manual that justified their treatment of me, no justice could happen. Most of these men who used me as a type of sexual experiment are now old. Maybe life has already avenged my treatment. My mother and aunt died mad and wanting answers. I wish I had provided them with closure before they died. But many years had passed, and I was now a mother of four and it did not look like there was anything that could have helped except an apology decades later. How do you force someone to apologise? I write this to tell my mother and aunt that I heard them. I am taking steps to claim back what was taken from me. I am truly sorry I never told them in time.

The apology would not have made a difference as that was a definite sexual assault by a church, of all things. They stripped me of my privacy and dignity, I had a right to self-determination. We all see things from different lenses and as a teenager, I had a right to have been seen by only my Bishop and a right to have made mistakes. They had a chance to apologise as they must have realised that no church manual approved this. Why was I the special and chosen one? I know for sure that I am the only female teenager in Mdantsane who went through this barbaric act that has lasted my lifetime and am not the only one who broke the law of chastity.

From that day that judgement was passed, I could not remember my dreams. I could not remember who I wanted to be. It feels as though I have been winging it. I can't have lasting relationships with men. I don't trust men. My life has been a series of improvisations. I used to have an idea of the kind of impact that I wanted to have on the world but with chronically stunted self-esteem, many doors were closed for me. A vicious cycle began that needed a multi-disciplinary approach. This included psychologists, psychiatrists, and occupational therapists.

When I moved to Durban for medical school, I had to find a Bishop to discuss this dilemma with. I had been instructed by the church to find a Bishop. His first and last impressions of me were that of a promiscuous teenager, which I was not. Even the boy in question had left me months back suggesting that being a Mormon was more important to me than anything else on earth and maybe that was what I needed to pursue. He had disappeared out of my life never knowing the repercussions that our so-called love had wreaked in my world. The new Bishop was kind and had many students as his members and that must have been hard for him. It took years before he lifted this punishment.

In hindsight, it was important to have developed a moral code as a teenager. In earnest, I did not know any better than that tea and coffee were bad and sex outside marriage was an abomination. Without those truths, I might have engaged in sexual escapades as an incredibly young teenager. Also, the fact that we had something called Seminary where we were taught all the scriptures every Friday after school truly helped. When I graduated from High School I also graduated from Seminary. The homework from Seminary was tough and our teacher could easily tell if we had copied from one another and so you had no choice but to do your work.

The friendships made would last a lifetime. I am grateful that I shared this piece of me with my support system: my dear aunt, and my beautiful mother. I had always thought that it would mean them rejecting me as the church rejected my imperfections. I remember overhearing them discuss that my mental problems dated long before the end of my marriage. They expressed how they now regretted the decision to have me, and my cousin baptised. At least no one else got baptised as children in my family again. Whatever injustices or blessings ended with me. I also paid back all the money that the bursary paid for the first two years before it was taken away, R12 000 to be exact.

A JUDGEMENT UNFAIRLY GIVEN – REPENTANCE

"In the depths of winter, I finally learned that within me there lay an invincible summer."
— Albert Camus

I would like to highlight two things for young teenagers who are trying to find themselves even within the Mormon church. The first is that experiences like mine will continue and this is the reason. My second husband converted to Mormonism just before we got married and because he is a learned man, he was given "callings." At one point, he was even given the role of the ward clerk and would sit in disciplinary hearings and some of these would include people who had broken the law of chastity, like me. When he was given these *callings,* he was never interviewed in terms of what he knew. They were just filling all the empty vacancies in terms of callings.

I had never even seen my husband read the Book of Mormon, yet he had big *callings*. No one cared how much he knew about this new church that he joined except that he had the appearance of a person who might know a couple of things. That does not suffice because my husband would come home and tell me everything. How was he expected to know manuals if he did not have the testimony of the Book of Mormon itself? No wonder he started drinking! All those Bishopric meetings probably contributed to stressing him out of his mind. He would even go to church smelling of alcohol and I would wonder if he was not doing it deliberately so that he was relieved of his duties. No one gave him a chance to explore if this was indeed his truth. I am sure that this practice of giving big callings like smarties continues all over the world—especially in third world countries— and we wonder why the retention rates are so poor.

The second thing is that you have a right, a human and social right, to not have to discuss sexual things with only men present. This is a danger and will continue to be so. As you grow, you will come short of perfection and that is okay. You will be okay. What happened to me was not only social injustice, but it was also a violation of my human rights and prejudice over me as a woman. My prayer is that you stand your ground more firmly than I ever did.

Repentance is a good thing, but it is important to allow your intuition to guide you and allow your relationship with your Maker to be your true foundation. Men will continue to be fallible.

THE DEATH OF MY MOTHER

"It is not impermanence that makes us suffer. What makes us suffer is wanting things to be permanent when they are not."
—Thich Nhat Hanh

From the Princess: Tears, Idle Tears
By Alfred Lord Tennyson[9]

Tears, idle tears, I know not what they mean,
Tears from the depth of some divine despair
Rise in the heart, and gather to the eyes,
In looking on the happy Autumn-fields,
And thinking of the days that are no more.

Fresh as the first beam glittering on a sail,
That brings our friends up from the underworld,
Sad as the last which reddens over one
That sinks with all we love below the verge;
So sad, so fresh, the days that are no more.

Ah, sad and strange as in dark summer
Dawns
The earliest pipe of half-awaken'd birds
To dying ears, when unto dying eyes
The casement slowly grows a glimmering square
So sad, so fresh, the days that are no more.

Dear as remember'd kisses after death,
And sweet as those by hopeless fancy feign'd
On lips that are for others; deep as love,
Deep as first love, and wild with all regret;
O Death in Life, the days that are no more!

I read the poem above by Alfred Lord Tennyson frequently. Before I cry over the death of the single most significant person in my life, I first laugh. It took a long time before my mom took the COVID-19 virus seriously. Just before lockdown, in March 2020, I had been admitted to a hospital in Cape Town and since we were admitted for mental health reasons we were advised on a discharge since we were not necessarily dying. They were worried that the airlines would close, and we might find ourselves stranded. At the airport, people were wearing masks and I quickly called home and told them to go to every pharmacy and acquire some masks. They told me that they were at the big mall in East London, and no one was wearing a mask and that I would be making fun of them. When I returned home I was unable to get masks from anywhere and I went to a kiddies' shop and got different masks that we could use until East London was safe again.

We moved into my beach house for a while because it was not crowded, also because our masks were scary to wear in public. We were wolves, superheroes, and all kinds of scary things. What seemed real was that SARS-CoV-2 (COVID-19) was now established. A lockdown was initiated, and people were dying. Around June 2020, my aunt Phumeza was admitted to the hospital. My driver was there, as always, to take care of my people. A few weeks thereafter, my mother started getting sick.

I was not aware my mother was sick since she felt that she was a doctor because she gave birth to one, and had gone to collect medications at my rooms, but I was also at home and had a trusted locum at my practice. She called me very early on a Saturday morning and told me that she had headaches that were not going away and that she had finished two packets of painkillers without any success. She was crying and I was drowsy and groggy from the sleeping pills from the night before and I told her that I would send Owen, the driver, to get her. I realised when I put the phone down that it was a Saturday and Owen would not be coming. I left home in my pyjamas and on my way I instructed my nurse to meet me at the practice.

I fetched my sick mother from her house and took her to the practice. I put up intravenous lines (IV lines) and started the megavitamin drips, Dexamethasone, Azithromycin and all the works. We were in between nebulisation and oxygen. She was looking a bit better when I left with her. She told me that she wanted to go to my house and sleep in a separate room. She instructed me to not tell the kids that she was there because she did not want to infect them, even though she had not yet tested. She was convinced that she had COVID-19. I kept nebulising, giving her oxygen, using the oximeter, and using the drips but my mom did not want to go to the hospital and was not showing any hard signs of improving. She was not well; she had established tachypnoea (rapid laboured breathing) and I had to assist her when she needed to go to the bathroom. She would keep telling me that we would go to the hospital the next day and that she did not want to be a burden to me. When the next day arrived she would say that she felt better, even though that was not true. I was not wearing a mask during this nursing of my mother. We spent the most meaningful times lying in that bed facing each other. I had no real understanding that these were my last moments with her. We spoke about everything under the sun. Our last moments together were closely bonded, informal, yet real. There were no apologies because we had made those many years ago, or months even—the fights of a daughter and her beloved mother.

She still looked stunningly perfect and right at the last moment, she agreed to go to the hospital. I sat with her in her hospital bed, and I cannot remember what was preoccupying my mind. We did X-rays and went back to her bed. I think it was dawning on me that I also had COVID-19. I had not used any precautions while caring for my mother... It was time for me to call Dr Onke Tshiki.

Onke had been my best friend since the first day of medical school. The only man I have ever met who has never disappointed me. My eldest child was fourteen and even though, I have trustees, only Onke will be willing to take my children in the event of my death. COVID-19 was knocking hard on my door and for a moment I realised that I might not make it. I had to start planning for the future of my children because a future without me was beckoning. Yes, I still had two aunts and two cousins but only Onke knew me and my idea of parenting by that time. Onke had been my constant for as long as I can remember. I remember once telling him that it seems so unfair to continue living a life I no longer had any interest in living. He always knew how to reach the sub-atomic particles of my demented mind. He is a psychiatrist now who even as a medical student could read my soul, thus we called each other soulmates. He was aware of the traumas caused by the death of Nombuyiselo and the post-traumatic events with the church council. It was truly sublime to watch Onke take over and do the work of reassuring me and helping me get through all the hurdles that were in my way. Onke continues to be the single most important person in my life apart from my children. He makes me feel as though I matter, that I have so much to offer still. He sees me in a way that even I don't see myself. Yes, granted he was no magician, but he was there for me and always has been.

His treatment of me reminds me of the book *Falling Upward* by Richard Rohr. Rohr gives a beautiful tribute to life in Japan post World War Two. There was a custom that was designed to reintegrate the lives of the soldiers back into community life. During the ritual, the soldier was publicly thanked and praised for his service to his country and his community, and this was said over him, "The war is now over! The community needs you to let go of what has served you and served us well up to now." Rohr calls it discharging your loyal soldier in his work with men. This ritual felt so apt in the way Onke systematically dealt with my problems and allowed me the space to dream again. To think and fixate on the past and things that I could change no longer.

The process of letting go would start and stop over the years but its truth and reality have been entrenched in me. It is okay to start and stop. The seed had been planted and mine was to discharge my loyal soldier. This process was not easy and took and time and in fact, you could call me a work in progress. Julia Cho in her blog '*Studies in Hope*' also explored this concept and the institution of rituals. I am a very ritualistic person and even at the end of my marriage, I performed a ritual to mark its end.

Just as I had predicted, I tested positive for COVID-19 a day or two after my mother's admission. I was so sick and was also admitted. My whole body was so painful. Talking felt like the most unattainable struggle on earth. Feeding myself was a mission not to be attempted in these pages. I remember when I first woke up, I asked the nurses for my rings. I thought I was married and had a husband who was waiting for me. I thought the nurses had stolen this husband like the second husband who was stolen by many hearts of different girls and women. I then thought cell phones were bombs. I would have caused an even worse debacle if I could move, but delirium had me in its grip.

My mother was admitted for eight days and died whilst the doctors were attempting to extubate her and transfer her to a C-PAP (Continuous Positive Airway Pressure) machine. By the time she died, I was recuperating at home following my own discharge. I had been blessed with a mother for thirty-nine years of my life. Now when I chronicle my life, there is the time when I had a mother, and the time when my mother died. She was buried three days later, and if only I had known it was our last time, I would have asked the gods to take me in her place. I would have gone down to the god Hades in Erebus to find and fetch her, even in the darkest places. I would have made Hades laugh as he is described in mythology by E.M. Berens as the god without a smile or laugh, even though he looked a lot like his brother Zeus. I would have thanked her for the life she gave me, for the parts of her that continue to live inside me—her courage, strength, beauty, and loyalty. I am yet to admit when I am wrong the way my mom did. I would have begged God to return her to my children who continue to pine for her. I would have chosen to leave in her place with all my ancestors that had gone before her, she was and continues to be needed. We are trying though to find some balance of normality even though the dishes she and my aunt made are second to none. That sadly is a reality and truth we have no choice but to live with for the rest of our lives.

A few days later my aunt also passed away. So, we buried her the following Saturday. They were more than just sisters; I used to call them twins and best friends as they were never apart. My support structure and my children's other mommies. They are missed not just by me, but by my grieving children and their brother and two remaining sisters. We will never forget them. They live on in our hearts forever. We look forward to the day we are reunited with them.

I needed to sit Shiva for my mother. Shiva is a Jewish custom that lasts for seven days and represents the mourning period in Judaism. It is a time when people have time to talk about their loss and comfort each other and be comforted by others. You sit Shiva for close people like a parent, a spouse, or a child who has passed away. The people sitting Shiva eat simple meals, and the day is spent sitting. This process can be traced to biblical times and for someone who is as ritualistic as me, I had always known I would sit Shiva for all my loved ones.

In the Bible after the death of Jacob, his son Joseph and those accompanying Joseph observed a seven-day mourning period. In the Book of Job, it was stated that Job mourned his misfortune for seven days.

Following Shiva is sheloshim which is thirty days of mourning. It is not strict as Shiva as people can leave their homes.

During the process of Shiva, only the memories and good times remained and even now as I face challenges that have to do with her death, I try to not lose sight of the wonder that she will always continue to be. Shiva reminded me that what we share is forever and was the first stage in my healing process. I sat Shiva with significant people in my life and I hope that it was as meaningful an experience for them as it was for me. I wish that there had been enough time to sit the entire period of Sheloshim. It was COVID-19 and children needed to be looked after and assisted as well in their grief.

The following words are written on my mother's tombstone:

LUTHANDO: You were the best granny anyone could ever ask for, you are in a good place, we will always miss you.

AZA: To the woman that raised me and loved our family like no other, I'll always miss and love you now and always, your little Ozie.

ZIKHONA: Best epipelagic and mesopelagic times, gratitude for support during my abyssal times. I only wish I had held your hand during your hadalpelagic zone. I love you.

As I sat in silence during Shiva, I was suddenly reminded of Kisa Gotami, from a Buddhist Parable. Kisa had married an only son of a very wealthy family and after their son was born, her life was complete and filled with unparalleled joy. Unfortunately, the boy died, and she refused to accept the demise and carried the child from house to house seeking a remedy. She was advised to seek medication from Buddha and off she went to Gautama carrying her dead child in her bosom. Upon meeting Buddha, he promised to bring her child back to life if she only brought back some mustard seeds so that he could make a remedy to bring her child back to life. However, there was a catch, she was supposed to get the mustard seeds from houses that had not experienced pain or loss of loved ones. She went on her quest only to meet people who were willing to assist her but had lost loved ones and had been met with hardships. At last, after not finding a single family that had not suffered loss, she summoned enough courage to leave her dead son in the forest and returned to the Buddha and told him that people are telling her that there are fewer people alive than the ones that are dead. She was taught about impermanence. This involved her accepting loss and finding meaning in it through entering her first path.

My mother had died, and we had both known that we would be separated someday. It is the way of life and there was no mustard seed to bring her back. Mine is to honour her memory and let her live on through me and my children. I realised a few months later that my grandmother died when my mom was thirty-nine years old and coincidentally I was also thirty-nine years old when I lost my mother. It still baffles me, but it's the truth and I feel the pain she felt at my age. Life is truly bewildering.

CHAPTER 4:

MY SECOND HUSBAND

"I remember the bright stars that shone above us on the night I fell in love with you. They somehow symbolised our forever. It was written for us long before we made commitments to one another. Ours was supposed to be an Eternal story. I know this because of the ache that has become a part of me."
—Zikhona Hlalempini,
21 September 2019 Journal entry

I would be lying if I told you that my husband and I had a fairy-tale meeting where it was love at first sight. This was the case for two iconic South African writers, Ingrid Jonker and André Brink. Even though both were married when they met, their love story would span a long time and would redefine what love meant to each of them as described in Ingrid's poetry collection called *Black Butterflies*. Ingrid dedicated numerous poems to André and even though their love affair would not last, its effects did. It was a true rollercoaster of a relationship whose depth exceeds that of many marriages.

I love how André describes its state of impermanence, he writes, "Time and time again we would break up, sometimes with a whimper, often with a bang. Time and time again, we would dive back into the love which beckoned like a dark and dangerous current. It could not possibly last." It reminded me a lot of my mother's marriage as it was always volatile, with many absences. I remember as an intern attending a play that was titled, *Remembering you like something I had forgotten*. Some aspects of Ingrid's life were explored in this play, including her suicide. I have been a fan of this great Afrikaner poet ever since.

When I met the love of my love I was an intern struggling through not just the strains of an internship in the Pietermaritzburg Complex but also a failing young marriage that had a son. My son was young, and I was uncertain about the future. I met my husband early in 2007 in a mall called Cascades when I went to hire a movie at the video shop where he worked. It is amazing how those are almost extinct in 2021. He later told me that he was the one who opened my account and even that encounter made no real impression on me. I had real problems and had no real answers or solutions to my problems except for knowing that I was trapped with a first husband who had told me he had tenders and a trust fund left to him by his long-dead father, only to learn that the Holy Ghost had told him to tell me these lies. I don't even remember any real apologies as I was now being supported by my mother, even though I was a married woman.

It so happened that towards the end of 2007 my family had come to visit. I lost my handbag while on call at work, during those 24-hour shifts taken by doctors during weekends after 04:30 p.m. I was due to return a video and miraculously my bag turned up with no money or valuables, but my ID, drivers' license, and car keys were there. I was able to return the video. Before this, I had made a call to the video shop to report my stolen bag and the time it would take to return the video. When I got there this kind guy, who would be my husband, had bought me a slab of Top Deck chocolate. My family was over the moon and told me they had a great feeling about him.

By this time, I had separated from my first husband and was in full internship mode. He was six years younger than me and doing the second year of his accounting degree qualification which was towards becoming a chartered accountant. He had asked me on a date some months before and I had made the excuse that my back was sore on the day that we were supposed to meet. I did not want to embark on a relationship whilst my divorce was taking long to be finalised. We had no assets, money, or pensions. We just had the child and he had already decided that I would bring up the child alone. I asked him once to take the child since he was not paying any child maintenance. We are still waiting for his family to fetch the now grown-up child as he had promised he would instead of paying maintenance.

In as much as my mother wanted me to find love and be happy, she was fearful of relationships between married and unmarried persons. As a nine-year-old child, she would tell us often of an experience she encountered whilst coming back from school. She hated married men, if she could, she would have tattooed herself if, "If Married Please Do Not Talk to Me." This disdain worsened when a married person showed any love interest in her. It was like a declaration of war, and I never understood it till I went back to the story she used to tell us as children. She says she could hear voices and noises as she came closer and then suddenly she saw many people all carrying a whip or weapon. Inside this circle were two naked people, a man, and a woman. There people hurling insults kept explaining that the man was married and the woman unmarried and this was the punishment they received from being found in bed together. She must have been so confused as she did not even understand what being found in bed together meant. She has never felt safe around married men ever since, in her mind if you want to avoid disappointment, humiliation, and beatings, run when you see a married man.

She practised that her whole life and has often wondered if that couple lived. She put that impression in our minds to stay away from married men. Now the roles were reversed. I was still legally married and knew my first husband would ensure that it becomes a long and costly exercise to finalise the divorce. I had no choice but to go on with my life as I was not going to be controlled inside and outside marriage. The abuse inside the marriage was enough. The marriage that was doomed from the onset with a husband I was fearful of. I used to ask my mom to call me in the morning to ensure that I was still alive.

There was going to be a party on New Year's Eve on 31 December 2007 in Pinetown with my church friends and I invited the accountant from the video shop. This was a night to remember because this was the night that I fell for him. What a night, what a guy. Herein lay the magic, a thinker, a man I could talk to for an entire night till it became morning and still want to talk some more. We slept in my car when we could not find a bed and breakfast and that was okay. We were concerned only with each other and listening to Maria Callas. He knew literature too. How was that even possible? He recited many lines of significant pieces as I studied his face. I was in heaven.

We decided to go on a date the following day. I do not remember where we went, but I remember being terrified of leaving the car when we got to the destination. When he asked why I told him I feared making memories. In hindsight, it must have been my intuition. I think we experience these fears but decide they are of no consequence. I made that mistake too. Something told me that I shouldn't make these memories. Was it a premonition of the hell that would be unleashed a decade later? Was it my dead father, dead cousin and dead grandparents who could already see what effects this union would have on me? Suddenly, it dawned on me that we were making a memory, the formal date where it was just the two of us.

My love for him was perfect. It had cured so many imperfections, so much pain, and had covered so many insecurities. I could draft books on waking up next to him and touching his face. Then kissing him like it was something I had done for as long as I had been alive. This was a love story, a perfect love story. I fell head-over-heels in love with my husband. My systems, my organs, my cells, my mitochondria, my nuclei, my molecular self, my atomic self, my sub-atomic selves all fell in love. He had a fingerprint detection to my heart. He needed no keys. His prints were enough to awaken me from even the deepest sleep and without him next to me, sleep almost became non-existent. When he returned, he would always know that I first needed to sleep. We would go straight to sleep because this man was my constant, my sleeping pill, my everything, even my God. Without him nothing made sense, nothing mattered. I had never felt more alive than when he was next to me. I just needed more of him, more of this love, this love was everlasting.

After this encounter, we were blessed with many encounters and had the kind of relationship that spanned almost ten years. I loved him and I wanted to shout this truth over mountain tops for the world to see, to hear, to witness that the kind of love we have exists. He took me to Durban for our first Valentine's Day together and it was an experience that was out of this world. We went to the ocean and watched the sunset as the ocean returned to his wife, the beautiful copper-like sky. We ate, danced, and were just so drunk in love. His voice sounded like it came from heaven itself, it was simply perfect, so was he. I had never imagined that love could feel this good.

The River-Merchant's Wife: A Letter
By Ezra Pound[10]
After Li Po

While my hair was still cut straight across my forehead
I played about the front gate, pulling flowers.
You came by on bamboo stilts, playing horse.
You walked about my seat, playing with blue plums.
And we went on living in the village of Chōkan:
Two small people, without dislike or suspicion.

It Can Turn

At fourteen I married My Lord you.
I never laughed, being bashful.
Lowering my head, I looked at the wall.
Called to, a thousand times, I never looked back.

At fifteen I stopped scowling,
I desired my dust to be mingled with yours
Forever and forever, and forever.
Why should I climb the look out?

At sixteen you departed
You went into far Ku-tō-en, by the river of swirling eddies,
And you have been gone five months.
The monkeys make sorrowful noise overhead.

You dragged your feet when you went out.
By the gate now, the moss is grown, the different mosses,
Too deep to clear them away!
The leaves fall early this autumn, in wind.
The paired butterflies are already yellow with August
Over the grass in the West garden;
They hurt me.
I grow older.
If you are coming down through the narrows of the river
Kiang;
Please let me know beforehand,
And I will come out to meet you
As far as Chō-fū-Sa.

I could taste the essence of his love and as the above poem illustrates, my only wish and desire was for my dust to be mingled with his forever and forever and forever. It was everything that I had read in books and so much more. Nothing in my life had prepared me for that moment, for this love. In the poem, the husband leaves for war and is severely missed by his wife who grows even jealous of paired butterflies. I had always thought that, like this poem, only an unpreventable calamity would separate us. I never saw myself without him as the lady in this poem, hurting and growing old alone. My assumptions were wrong because in less than ten years together, I would be growing alone without him. Growing old without the love of your life feels like a life sentence for a crime you never committed, but you will do the time anyway.

My husband was dark and short, had a significantly chipped tooth that fell off when he bit into an apple when he was younger. He always had a book in his hand, some science fiction book. He had already read the *Game of Thrones* long before it became a worldwide hit. He taught me the different signals and what they stood for, and I just sat there and watched his serious face. He also taught me how to work at the video shop as I wanted to spend as much time as possible with him. My doctor friends found it odd that my part-time work was at a video shop. They had no idea I was there for love, and I

111

was not even getting paid. He was brilliant, a valedictorian in his high school.

When I consider how he assisted me with how I viewed myself, it was almost miraculous. My self-esteem was at an all-time low and my peers could not understand this as we had just been bestowed new titles—we were doctors! All our dreams were about to come true. They call it delayed gratification, right? We had watched people we went to high school with not only buy cars but homes as well. But still, with all this futurity that seemed so certain, I had demons. Not only was my divorce from my first husband taking forever and charging an arm and a leg, but I also fell pregnant. I was not sure how to feel about this development. I told my mother as she was the only person that I trusted, but I was not sure about what the pregnancy would do for a still married person who was an intern. I had just made my problems worse, but this pregnancy would teach me something so profound about the soul I had inside me.

My husband had a family that used a healer that used methods I had not seen before. When we went for a consultation, I was instructed to lie on a bed and this white lady stood above me with a pendulum that swung back and forth until I became drowsy. This a divination tool in spiritual healing and had put me in a meditative state by aligning my energy centres. All this was new to me as I had only known Joseph Smith and the Book of Mormon as points of reference in spirituality. Everything about this lady was kind, truthful, sincere, and even a mind as scientific as mine made room to understand her truths. When I woke up I sat across her on her consulting table, and she had a message from my unborn child. This was strange because it was a very early pregnancy, five days or so. I had blood tests taken to confirm it. My body is very strange in that I can tell I am pregnant from conception. My breasts become excruciatingly painful, and I usually go straight for the blood test.

We had not told her about the pregnancy, yet she had a message for me from the baby that I was carrying and informed me that my child was a boy. She told me that my beautiful baby had told her that he understood that I was very conflicted by the pregnancy and that a lot was happening in my life. He further told me that if his continued growth inside me was an impediment, he understood and all I had to do was tell him that I am not ready to have him, and he would abort. He would do this because he loved me and did not want to see me suffer. This kind lady further explained that this custom of talking to the grown-up soul of your unborn child was very popular among Red Indians and that is how they have aborted or miscarried for centuries.

I never wanted to abort my baby boy. To this day he continues to make me proud. He is twelve years old now and I have told him this story and it still blows his mind. If someone had told me this I would have never believed them, being the sceptic that I am.

I gave birth to my son in January 2009. He weighed only 2.2 kg and was pale and yellow like my son before him. This one was so tiny. I wanted to kangaroo mother him for the rest of his life. His little life was already a story of resilience. I feel like a spectator when I watch his accomplishments and his life and wonder what we could have done so right to be blessed with a champion.

My husband moved to East London in October 2009 after having completed his honours' degree. He became an article clerk in one of the big audit firms and our life was on the right track. We rented a beautiful three-bedroomed house in Bonnie Doon and had one car, a red Alpha Romeo, which was followed by a Toyota Fortuner a few years later. Life seemed perfect, it felt like we were cheating, that we were in an open book exam, and we were always winning. Our major hurdle after having a child in 2009 was that I struggled to fall pregnant. This was a source of great sadness for us. After going to so many doctors we made the plan of adopting as the idea of In-vitro Fertilisation seemed too costly.

We got married in July 2011 and people still find it hard to believe the way it happened. We had taken leave from work because we wanted to go on a getaway to

Durban for five days. What we had not envisaged was that my son was going to get Meningitis for the third time earlier in the week. It became clear that with a sick baby it was going to be difficult to go on holiday. So, on Thursday, we woke up with a sense of purpose and wanted to tick off some things that needed to be done and we realised that one of those things was getting married. We googled and found someone willing to marry us for a cost of R600, we were elated as it was so nice and cheap. I called my family, and they all came and off we went to Cintsa. It was at a church opposite the Lilyfontein school. We were married by the humblest man I have ever met, and he assured us that our marriage was going to last.

He told us that he had experienced only one divorce in his life as a marriage officiator and the wife was mentally unwell, and this news brought about so much peace in my life. Often when people marry, it is acceptable for them to vow, "till death do us part." My first marriage was in the temple and the temple the words said are, "for time and all eternity." Even though I was marrying a man that I had loved with all my heart, I knew that my fate was tied to my first husband for time and all eternity. I wondered who my husband would represent to me in eternities, would he just be the father of my children? Would we be allowed to kiss since our marriage ended during death? When I die, I automatically become the wife of someone I did not like that much. This was a tragic thought. Divorcing eternally is a long and strenuous process that is done in America, where the headquarters of the church is located and only the prophet himself can grant that divorce. I have a feeling though, that right now in 2021, he is no longer my husband eternally. We have all gone through a lot in life, even him. I think I am finally free from him.

My second husband passed both the exams that qualified him as a chartered accountant. We started the process of adopting our third baby. He was born on 6 December 2013, and this was the year before we bought our house. The administrative papers that go into the adoption process were tremendously long and tedious but finally, we were done. We went to court within a year and our son was ours forever. What we had not known was that I was going to fall pregnant the following month and our children would be ten months apart. It was not easy raising forced twins, but it became the blessing I had never asked or prayed for. They are best friends and I love them with all my heart. They are now seven and eight years old and are starting to have different interests, but they remain each other's allies.

We watched our children reach their milestones and were delighted with the progress at school of our oldest two boys. Life was truly marvellous. We had started on this course of a life together and it was working, but like

Narnia, all would be threatened and a new life forged but not before we embarked on numerous journeys. We went on holiday, mostly with my mom and aunt looking after our youngest children. We would sometimes be joined by my uncle. We drove or flew to most towns in South Africa and had beautiful international vacations. I have kept all the pictures for the sake of remembrance.

We went on holiday so many times that we went to other places more than once. These places included Hogsback; a beautiful village situated in the Amathole Mountains of the Eastern Cape Province. It is filled with indigenous forests, waterfalls, and beautiful exotic plants. There is something primal and exciting about this village that you become lost in its splendour. We once experienced a marvellous Christmas in July when I was pregnant with my daughter, and we built snowmen. It is not even in a coastal area, but it was our favourite place. We had our last holiday together here.

I have not been there ever since as it now holds a painful memory. A memory of when I realised that I would never see my husband the same way again. We had gone there to rethink our life together and start afresh, but there was no reset button, and the most heart-breaking thing was that I was not there and knew that our life together was over. He had cheated and I was just going through the motions as we were at Hogsback. I was never going to go back to him. It is not in my nature to understand big themes like cheating and disloyalty. I was hoping that all the tears of my family and his family could change my nature, but they didn't. We took a walk on the Labyrinth at The Edge which is one of the attraction sites in Hogsback. I was taken aback by its beauty and magnetic, artistic, and timeless influence. For a moment, the briefest moment, we were us again. I remembered falling for him and the preceding beautiful life we lived. Then as quickly as that image had appeared it had vanished again. We were over. The intricate series of pathways of the labyrinth were almost symbolic. It became evident to me that it would be too complicated to find each other in this maze.

THE DEATH OF FOREVER

One Art
By Elizabeth Bishop[11]

The art of losing isn't hard to master; so many things seem
filled with the intent
To be lost that their loss is no disaster.

Lose something every day. Accept the fluster
of lost door keys, the hour badly spent.
The art of losing isn't hard to master.

Then practice losing farther, losing faster:
Places, and names, and where it was you meant to
Travel. None of these will bring you disaster.

I lost my mother's watch. And look! my last, or
next-to-last, of three loved houses went.
The art of losing isn't hard to master.

I lost two cities, lovely ones. And, vaster,
some realms I owned, two rivers, a continent.
I miss them, but it wasn't a disaster.

—Even losing you (the joking voice, a gesture
I love) I shan't have lied. It's evident
the art of losing's not too hard to master
though it may look like (Write it!) like a disaster.

When I was a medical student something spectacular happened in Durban: four monks arrived and built a mandala for many gruesome painstaking hours. They were silent throughout the process, and it was a sight that I will remember for as long as I live. I wondered about how uncomfortable and painful their bodies must have been as they toiled to create this masterpiece. I had no idea that mandalas are mostly destroyed, and that their creation is that of fulfilling a purpose. The structure they had built was so serene, so beautiful, so peaceful, so enchanting that I thought it would last forever like the Pyramids of Giza. However, in a matter of hours, this structure was destroyed. It had been a sand mandala and its significance was to highlight the importance of enjoying whatever beauty life gives us and its subsequent impermanence. We were taught about the transitory nature of life and as Elizabeth states in the above beautiful poem, that loss is not such a terrible thing. You can lose cities, keys, and the love of your life and remain standing. It is not a disaster but making these losses the theme song of your life, now that is a disaster.

I can't tell you the exact date when my husband stopped loving me, but something was brewing—a gut feeling, an intuition, it was there. It was in the way he looked at me. I used to feel like his Helen of Troy, the face that launched a thousand ships. He started looking at me with disdain and disgust as if he asked himself how he ended up with me. He had access to so many stiletto-wearing and weave-stitching women. He would beg me to look like this. I was a doctor and a mother to four children with a constantly travelling husband and there was little time for weaves, let alone stilettos. My mom never taught me how to walk in these in any case.

The way I would wear my full underwear in front of him and sometimes ask for help to get my bottom underwear up, used to be normal, but it suddenly became unsexy. He started taking more than six sinusitis tables before going to bed and antihistamines are sedating by nature. My mother once commented that he took all these tablets so that he didn't have to deal with me, and I remember thinking that was the most hurtful thing my mother had ever said to me. He would be asleep when I got back from the practice. It started the year he became a chartered accountant.

He changed drastically in the year that he moved to a job that provided a lot of travelling opportunities. He became odd but very friendly towards colleagues. He was arrogant, I had loved that about him but now he was everybody's best friend and no longer my person. I could feel his essence, it was not of a person who was in love with me anymore. I remember a work function that he had invited me to sometime in the last two years of our marriage. We were having a conversation with his bosses and friends who kept asking him about Michaelhouse and the experience of having been both a student and now an alumnus. They asked me questions too of whether we were taking our sons to the same school as their father. A lady I went to high school with was the main instigator of these questions. She was in awe that I snatched the real deal. He answered all the questions calmly and was asked about people who may have studied there around the same time. I don't even think my husband has ever entered the gates of Michaelhouse. It has been the first or second most expensive school in South Africa for decades. Never had I been so humiliated and embarrassed on his behalf. He was already a chartered accountant, something very few people will ever attain, but he had to lie about his past. Why his past? Why did it matter which high school he went to? Why would he put me in such an uncomfortable situation without giving me a heads up that people here believed he was from Michaelhouse?

When I watched Frozen 2, Olaf started melting because Elsa had gone too far in finding the source of her powers, her freezing feature was dying and so was she. I could relate to what Olaf felt when he said that he was flurrying. He could see and feel himself drifting and that's how I felt. My husband was drifting, he was flurrying away. He sometimes said that he was adopted, and other times would say that he was fostered by the family that his mother worked for. He chose to stay with this family and replace his mother and siblings. He felt that his true siblings were the white family that made him wake up at the wee hours of the morning throughout his childhood to make them coffee because they were too scared of hiring someone who might have HIV. He never mentioned a word was about his black family to people. This was the situation I lived with—a man who had the most profound existential crisis I have ever known.

The fights became frequent. He became more irritable and restless whenever I became needy. My family must have irritated him the most as he kept commenting that if we were to separate, I would still have a support system unlike him whose parents were both dead. He complained endlessly about my mother and my aunt, that my mother did not respect him even though she cooked, cleaned, and washed for him. I learnt first-hand the ingratitude of people. My husband had forgotten about the suit that my mother and aunt had borrowed for him for his first interview as an article clerk. He changed the clothes in a communal toilet in a filthy section of Mdantsane named the Highway.

The first incident that should have warned me that all was not well happened when I was pregnant with my daughter around July 2014. We had applied for a bond to buy a house and it was approved. We were over the moon with excitement. We decided to have dinner with our two sons at a very classy and stylish restaurant called

Grazia. When I got to the venue I made a conscious decision to leave my phones in the car because this was a momentous family occasion, and I did not want to be disturbed by messages or phone calls. My husband, on the other hand, chose to have his phone on him the whole time we were there. Although I knew his password, his phone was invariably nowhere to be found but with its owner, even at 02:00 a.m. if he got up to pee, he had his phone with him.

There was a message on his phone that he thought I did not see, and he quickly turned to something else. He told me some lame excuse, but my peripheral vision had done me a favour for once in its existence, I could see not only the message but the name of the person who sent it. The message was inappropriate as were the many that would follow years later. Even on a trip, we had to Hong Kong, my husband was a hero to his girls in South Africa and I watched their thankful hearts and kissing emojis as they were indeed grateful that their blesser had not abandoned them even when he was outside the country.

We were with children on the restaurant episode, and I did not want to deal with this shock in front of them, so I waited. When we got home, we had no electricity and he had to rush to the garage. He left his precious companion, his phone, behind by mistake. I looked at the messages. By the morning they were erased. This made me aware that my beautiful husband had some inappropriate relationship with this person and instead of fighting, I went home and did not even tell my mother. I pretended to be too tired to drive home as I needed to process this new development. Was I now going to be a single mother? What was the worst that could happen?

We eventually discussed this, and I got to talk to the apologetic lady who had been going through a break-up and my husband was there to catch her fall. Who would catch me? It was now established in my mind that there was a problem with my husband, but I made myself believe that it was a lesson that he had learnt and that in the future he would consider me before embarking on weird relationships with unmarried conflicted women who needed a shoulder to cry on. That was a terrible assumption because this was not even the beginning. There were stories I heard about that dated before this incident.

Our bedroom was on the second floor of our house. There was a door to a passageway next to our room which led to the indoor stairs that led to the roof. We had numerous parties on the roof. It was heavenly. There were windows instead of a concrete wall between our room and the passage. The house is old and the architecture questionable. We had little privacy as the kids could come in through the second door when they would hear raised voices. Another anomaly about our bedroom was that we did not have proper ventilation windows because the ones I have just described were contained in that space. So, we had a huge sliding door behind our headboard and when opened, some fresh air could come through. We made the mistake of building a pool instead of making the house safer for us and the children. We had no security gate which meant that anyone could have fallen. We made sure that the kids did not play in our bedroom and as a result, we never had an incident.

I had never imagined that my husband would start a new ritual of pushing me around and dragging me towards the open sliding door. I would have to hold on to the different ends of the bed to prevent myself from falling out. He did this more than once and did it in front of my relative, helper, and children at one stage. During this encounter, he was dragging me outside and my brother-in-law arrived. I now suffer from terrible rotator cuff tendinitis in both my shoulders from the severity of being dragged by him. I did not share this with anyone for a long time, because I was too strong and educated to be a victim of domestic abuse, but I had to deal with it in therapy. I thought being dragged was not domestic abuse. I thought the humiliation was not such a big issue until my mind forced me to acknowledge the lie that was my marriage. You do not drag someone you love just because you no longer want them. You don't open the sliding door and scare them into thinking that they would fall from the second floor.

If only my eldest son had not watched these acts from the window, he would not suffer from such horrible panic attacks, insomnia, and anxiety with vomiting every night, despite being on medication. He still thinks I am going to die and that I am all he has. Domestic violence is real; do not make excuses for it. The last time he pushed me around and dragged me, I fought back. I fought with so much strength that I was willing to die in the process. Coincidentally this last day of pushing me around was the last day of our marriage.

Early in 2013, we had decided to stay in Mdantsane which is where my practice is located. We had just the two oldest boys and saved money because renting in town was just too expensive. I had a friend from church who had passed away and his sister had asked me to ask my husband for help in accounting. She must have been in grade 10. I begged my husband to help her as he was not very interested. Little did I know that she would become obsessed with my life and that of my husband. She would call at all hours, even when we had moved, and because she was so young I had assumed it was about accounting. Years later I would learn about Bed and Breakfast bookings between the two of them while being taught 'Accounting.' My aunt's insurance had traced a phone to her. My aunt had given my husband a phone which he never used but gave to his girlfriend and it had suddenly disappeared. There was also an incident where this child broke the windscreen of my red car, and according to my dear husband, it was a Hadada ibis bird that had caused this accident. All the revelations were conversations they exchanged with each other over social media. The girl later posted pictures that showed she was in my ex-husband's place after we had separated. She is no longer with him right. The message for young girls is that grown men are after your youth. They know their types and the people they want to settle down with. Get an education and prioritise your future.

We would host parties where he would invite girlfriends. I was able to verify this after I found the phone numbers from all the cash send bank statements. The last party was strange; I had Tonsillitis on Sunday and started an antibiotic that made me have very bad diarrhoea. The diarrhoea and Tonsillitis were killing me, and we were going to have his party on Saturday. The runny tummy was getting worse every day and sometimes it would just run before I had enough time to run to the toilet. He did not change any of the bedsheets, instead, he would torture and ridicule me as if he did anything to help. I had an incredible helper who saw I was sick and would put all soiled things aside.

Even on the day of the party, he had invited his Nando's girlfriend. I was still very sick, but my friends helped me change constantly. On his cash send reference, my husband would write "investment" as a reference and the phone number would be on the statement. When I asked why he bothered to write *investment*, he answered that he was investing in sleeping with them in the future so that they don't become difficult when that time came. He could not think of anything that would sound more palatable to say.

Just when I thought that things couldn't get worse or weirder, I called one of the numbers on the bank statements and the lady on the other side asked me not to ask her about a man who had also slept with her best friend. This was a man clearly trapped in a marriage that he no longer wanted. I had finished serving my purpose of assisting him to become his dream self, and my reward was a man who cheated on me more than twenty times. This was my payment for being six years older.

In our first consultation with a psychologist, he mentioned that I forced him to adopt our beloved son. Mind you, he is the one who was brought up by a white family that fostered him. I had grown up with my mother till the age of thirty-nine. I thought the adoption was really for him, a chance to give back. How could I have forced him to fill and sign so many pages?

There were many incidents including cheating and him attempting to take his life in full view of everyone.

When he first attempted committing suicide, using the blue methylated spirit I was using to clean the umbilical area of my second infant baby, I should have recognised traits of instability. His reasons for attempting this parasuicide were because he did not feel that I was concentrating on him enough since the very tiny baby was born. Instead, he was now vomiting blood and calling me so that my attention could be shifted from the baby to him. It is amazing how we see so much of our situations and decide not to see them for what they are and what they represent. I had married a man who had his demons and when they manifested themselves I made excuses till the time came for me to find the courage to let go, even if that courage came at the cost of great mental distress.

A week after all the revelations, I formulated the idea that if I did the same thing then we could both forgive each other. I called my first boyfriend after days of trying to get his number. More than the cheating I did with him if you call it cheating since I never hid the fact that I was looking for his numbers to my husband. To inflict pain on my husband, I gave him my boyfriend's HIV results so that he knew that I would not use a condom with the other guy. This boyfriend was there for me even though he was in the process of burying his father and was in obvious grief. He helped me make sense of my life and since he loved working on cars, he would do that the entire day as I sat contemplating my next move. I will never forget helping him carry those engines even though I had no idea what he was doing with them. It was a safe space as this was an old friend, an old ally.

I think this cheating stint sealed our fate. From then on I was the bigger sinner in our so-called marriage. I truly didn't care; I had long been replaced anyway. Our marriage was truly over, and I knew it. My husband knew it.

I relayed this story of the open cheating to my therapist who told me that it was an act out of great pain. I did not want to be a victim and chose to cheat as well so that I did not have to be the only one doing the forgiving. Years later I realised that the act was not me. I had no idea what to do with all the emotions that were coursing through my veins. They were too confusing, too vast, and too rash. I did not even tell my mother about this part of my story as it happened. I did tell her eventually and she said that she had not known about this way of dealing with pain and being cheated on. It was my pain, I dealt with it the best way I knew how to deal with things. I fought back and would deal with the consequences at a later stage.

WHAT WAS LEFT BEHIND

You Left Me, Sweet, Two Legacies
By Emily Dickinson[12]

You left me, sweet, two legacies, —
A legacy of love
A Heavenly Father would content,
Had he the offer of;

You left me boundaries of pain
Capacious as the sea,
Between eternity and time,
Your consciousness and me.

Putting losses into words that others can understand is a daunting and challenging task. It needs to be attempted no matter how laborious it is. My children lost a full-time father who slept at home every day when he was not travelling. They lost those conversations they had with their father when he drove them to school. The atmosphere in our house was different because of a permanent change. There was no specific day when dad would return as during the time he was a husband and father to us. Father and son camps soon became extinct because I could not change my gender and become a father even though my children would beg to go to these sleep-over camps. Grieving, sad, and confused children who were acting up were left behind. Watching their friends that still had intact families was horrible for them and, more than anything, the confusion and sadness in their little faces was so evident.

Indeed, they were left with boundaries of pain as the above poem communicates so well, and as their mother, I could only provide a safe space to do the work of grieving. The only person who has put my children's sense of loss into a more coherent unit must have been Alfred Lord Tennyson when he said, "So sad, so strange, the days that are no more."

When I think of what was left behind in my family unit and a marriage that was now gone forever I cannot help but be reminded of the Koonalda cave on the edge of the Nullarbor Plain on a remote part of Australia. As you journey deep into the cave, an ancient underworld greets you. Deep underground there are soft rocks with markings on them that resemble hands. The artwork represents some of the oldest Aboriginal engravings in Australia and what has often fascinated me about these 20 000-year-old drawings was the intended messages behind them. Is there some code there that is relevant today of what they left behind for us? For future generations to know and take care not to ever traverse such paths? I thought often about these when dealing with the end of my marriage and what marks have been left behind to prove that a marriage had taken place and for a moment it was good, but only for the briefest moments.

What was left behind for me was mental health that took a turn and life of its own. I had to take different blood and urine samples to exclude any sexually transmitted diseases. The shame and embarrassment I felt when I went through such testing as a married woman was profusely enormous. I did a pap-smear with Human Papilloma Virus (HPV) genotyping (this test gives a probability of contracting cervical cancer) which is transmitted like HIV through sexual intercourse and this one can even be transmitted with oral intercourse, and this was the nail in the coffin. I tested positive for all subtypes which meant I had the highest risk for cancer of the cervix. Within a week I was in theatre having a total hysterectomy. This was a low point in my life. It was even lower than when my husband told me that he had fallen in love with a girl that works at Nando's, and they were not using condoms. I thought I could not go any lower, like Joseph in the Bible who had been thrown in a pit by his brothers, there I was also. My husband texted her the following words, "I love you more than you will ever know." But no, there was a lower point than that one when I had urinated in the bed at night after having my second c-section and he kept relating that story and demeaning me for it every time we fought as if he had even washed the bedding. We were staying at home with my mother, and she took care of everything.

The delirium that followed as I recuperated after the hysterectomy was out of this world. I was in and out of consciousness and it was terrible, there was no concept of time or presence, it was a dark cloud that enveloped every layer of me. To understand delirium, one would have to define it. It is usually described as a sudden change in a person's mental function, this may include thinking, behaviour, and levels of consciousness. This has some impairment to memory and concentration. I believed that we were in a submarine and that some secret agency like the CIA was coming to fetch us. In another episode of delirium, cell phones were bombs awaiting detonation and no one was willing to evacuate with me. I felt it my duty to warn all the other people in the ward of the impending doom looming over us as I went from bed to bed stark naked because the most important thing was the message that I was delivering—hospital clothes would have to wait.

The nurses got hold of my mother who arrived within an hour because she lived in Mdantsane and assured me that she would tell the people to take her in my place. She had to come early every day with my aunt and uncle and leave late in the evening when I had fallen asleep, after a full day of telling me old Xhosa folklore stories which had a way of calming my demented and confused mind.

Recovering from the hysterectomy was a long painful process but I am glad that I was lucky to have had it before the COVID-19 pandemic. I had the full support of my family, and this was something I did not take lightly and will always be grateful for. They were there every single day and looked exhausted, but they did not know how to forsake me like the brothers of Joseph left him. My pit was impermanent and whilst inside the pit, I was not hearing sounds of my prices being negotiated as was the case with Joseph. In time, I was able to recover fully while he was sold into slavery. Again, an illustration of impermanence, Joseph died being the second most important person of his time while his brothers came to beg him for mercy. There is nothing that is not designed to pass. If it cannot pass, then there is nothing acceptance and finding meaning cannot resolve within our very selves.

I am a very ritualistic person and after some time it felt only appropriate to organise our household and run it as you would run a monarchy. The name of our house is House Amherst—after the town in Massachusetts America where Emily Dickson was born and died. I recited the above poem daily at the end of my marriage, and it brought me peace and became my mantra. The fact that an American poet born in 1830 could articulate my pain so eloquently and coherently was so astonishing to me. My pain was as capacious as the ocean and my entire house of cards had erupted and fallen right in front of my eyes. The vows we made when we got married were broken and, for me at least, irreversibly so. That is why that final trip was a form of farewell to the people we used to be within the relationship. A marriage reeked with disloyalty was not going to cut it, at least not for me. Our house was reorganised with each person given a role and rules detailed how we governed our monarchy so that it lives on. It continues to guide us even through the most challenging times.

We recently informed my third son that he was adopted. I think we handled it well as the team and monarchy that we are. He continues to thrive and enjoys Minecraft and at this stage of eight years old, understands just enough that a closed adoption means he might never meet his birth mother. He is aware that at the beginning of the adoption process, she had declined the normal procedure of a letter and a picture every year as is customary with all closed adoptions. I don't stop to dream though; in my dreams, my son meets his biological mother and his siblings. I was able to give him some useful piece of information that I hope will have meaning to him when he grows older, his biological mother was light in complexion, just the way he is. I hope that he becomes an asset and meaningful member of his biological family one day just like Joseph of old. His place in Amherst will be forever his, and his alone.

A ritual that was the most significant in letting go, finding acceptance, and meaning was that of creating a Jizo. Close relatives were surprised as to why a Jizo was necessary at the end of a marriage as most *Mizuko kuyo* rituals are usually created after a loss of a child through a miscarriage or abortion in the Japanese tradition. After about six months after the end of my marriage, I started researching ways and rituals of letting go, some included throwing your wedding rings into the ocean, others mentioned making your wedding rings into another type of jewellery and others included a fire ritual and letting lanterns or balloons into the air. I had read about the ritual of a Jizo some years back and it felt more appropriate for my circumstances.

A Jizo is a type of statue created when a child does not fulfil its role of sojourning to earth through abortion, miscarriage, and stillbirth. Jizō Bosatsu is a safe guardian, a Buddhist protector of women and children that can let the soul of that child pass to the other side. In my case, this had been my second marriage. I would never have agreed to this second try if I was not sure that it would last. I went into my marriage sure that this thing that we had created would last forever, that it was real, authentic, and had all the embellishments of perpetuity. My prayer was that my unfulfilled marriage could be sent to the other side. The Jizo I created was a tree. This tree symbolised the marriage that I had entered that I believed would last endlessly, just like a true Jizo, it represented a life that did not fulfil its fruition but still had been present, no matter how long.

I sat down outside and watched the tree grow for years, contrary to the life that stops during a child miscarriage or abortion. The most amazing thing that happened is that a time eventually arrived when I had to let go of the Jizo, like the soldiers in post-war Japan, it had served its purpose. The time for mourning had ended. Just like in any monarchy, a time for a new leader had come to pass. Beautiful memories were left behind. Beautiful children carry on the legacy of a life once started with only the best of intentions. Meaning had come about even at the greatest costs.

Finding meaning for me did not mean that I'd walk into this red convertible car with a beautiful scarf to cover my hair—just like a movie with an awesome soundtrack playing in the background to the sunset—it means instead of living for your pain, you decide to live despite the pain. You start to believe that the pain was meant for some purpose, and you soldier on even though everything may not be as it should. Meaning comes in bits and pieces. It is my unending hope and prayer that my children learn to follow the example that I have set for them, the example of caring and carrying on. If in a hypothetical world my husband would ask me if I have forgiven him for the cheating and all the lies that came with the cheating, and for the disintegration of our family life; I would tell him I forgave him a long time ago. I wish him love, wealth, happiness, and all that his heart desires. All the paths I have travelled since our marriage were for my good, I became a better person because of it. I know rock bottom and it has a way of humbling you. Humility for me came at a great price and that is my story, not his.

CHAPTER 5:

SPIRALLING MENTAL HEALTH

A BRIEF HISTORY OF MENTAL HEALTH IN SOUTH AFRICA

A beautiful journal article by Ingrid G. Farreras[13] on the history of mental illness explored various prehistoric concepts. Mental illness has been present throughout history although its development and advancement has been surprisingly ancient. Throughout history, three ideas of categorising mental illness were put forward: supernatural, somatogenic, and psychogenic factors. Supernatural factors include beliefs on demonic possession, curses, and sin. Somatogenic factors are believed to be originating from the body itself. This could be an illness, an imbalance in the brain or genetic inheritance. Psychogenic factors focus on maladaptive learnt associations and cognitions that may be derived from traumatic and stressful events. There are myriad examples throughout history that show that there were treatments done to the mentally ill even though real treatments would only come some centuries later. The pharmaceutical companies have made mental illness treatment options almost abundant in our times even though the side effects can be horrendous and dreaded. The problem is that you must keep trying till the right medicine works for you.

We know that Greek physicians rejected the supernatural aspect of this illness and Hippocrates (460-370) himself made great strides in separating superstition and religion from medicine. All this work attempted by Hippocrates and Galen (130-201) was soon threatened in the nineteenth century. More humane treatment was introduced for patients who presented with these strange symptoms during the late Middle Ages when economic and political turmoil threatened power. Terms like possession and witchcraft were dealt with in horrendous ways. Witch-hunting continued and witches were burnt at the stake, even though these may have been women with mental illnesses (Farreras, 2013).

Lynn Gillis[14] published an article in 2012 that speaks to the evolution of psychiatry in South Africa. This was titled, *The historical development of psychiatry in South Africa since 1652*. I quote this specifically because it is pertinent in our country and usually to understand the present and the future one must have a grip on the past.

Structures for the mentally challenged were built in South Africa as far back as the years 1674, 1699, and 1772. A new hospital was built under the British colonial government where there were spaces created for the 'lunatics' aside from the physically sick. The main problem with all these hospitals was overcrowding. There were no psychiatric diagnoses nor was there treatment available. These places were for keeping these people with unfamiliar behaviours away from the general population that seemed normal.

Mental illness as a disease was named only in the late nineteenth century and Psychiatry was a word that was created by a French physician in 1808. To circumvent overcrowding in Somerset Hospital, mental patients were transferred to Robben Island in 1808. Although it had been a convict asylum, it now housed lepers, lunatics, and the chronically ill. Valkenberg Hospital was built in 1892 to ease the burden of mental patients in Robben Island. The living conditions were appalling, and treatment included sedatives, hypnotics, bromides which were not properly administered in terms of dosages. All this was new and at least there was progress made in treatment availability.

A new day dawned as many hospitals were being built and the treatment of patients were more humane. Community involvement offered better hope in terms of the overcrowding as some were able to look after their families. There was a period during World War One when there was nothing new that came about except for the differences seen in soldiers returning from war and a new term, 'shell shock' was coined. I suspect this was post-traumatic stress disorder. Freud, Jung, and other psychodynamic psychiatrists made some strides, however small. Classifications of mental illness by Kraepelin, Bleuler and others assisted in putting different groupings and in defining some types of illness. The modern era started in the mid-twentieth century where psychiatric hospitals were able to give patients the following: outpatient clinics, a therapeutic team approach, social and community services, occupational therapy, rehabilitation, etc. Because of advancements in psychiatry by 1987, it had lost much of its stigma attached to its history.

Under the apartheid regime, it became mandatory to separate black and white patients. Separate facilities were done by force and the only thing that became a redeeming feature for the black population was the year 1994 when a new government came into power. Different drugs were founded with Chlorpromazine in 1955, Lithium in 1949 and after World War Two, psychiatry had a personality and world of its own. Special dedicated units were now established, including eating disorders, personality disorders, child and adolescent psychiatry, and geriatric psychiatry. Training for specialists also began and so did legislation that governed the psychiatric patient. Indeed, as a country, we enjoy the full benefits of a structured approach to mental care and as we advance to a better understanding we also try not to forget the past.

MY MENTAL SPIRAL

"Go placidly amid the noise and haste, and remember what peace there may be in silence"
—Max Ehrmann, Desiderata

If I could go back and redo something in my life, I would do it, without missing a heartbeat, this would be undoing all the memories my children have of a depressed mother who could not get out of bed for months on end. A mother who could not even take them to a shopping mall because she could hear all the conversations of people going about their business. I cannot give you a date and time of when my mental health simply deteriorated. I have a feeling though, that the story is far more complex and somehow my mind protects me from delving into its deeper truths. I know that almost immediately after my marriage ended, the ability to sleep disappeared and permanently so, as I continue to be on sleeping tablets or antidepressants with a sedative side effect. Sleep waved goodbye to me with huge chunks of my sanity and reasoning abilities. I also waved goodbye back to these important character traits along with my lucidity.

It had always been very important for me to maintain a lucid mind, mainly because I had met, on many occasions in my profession, people whose minds had been so fractured that they were a shadow of their former selves. In the hospital, nurses who knew these people who were now stark naked and exposing themselves for the world to see would whisper, "this lady used to be a school principal, a doctor, a lawyer..." When your mind decides it needs to take a break from you, it does not care what position you hold in society. It does not care about your self-respect or your loved ones. It simply exits the building. I have a profound understanding and have been a witness to people whose lucidity had fallen by the wayside, but as a sad turn of luck would have it, this was now my turn at it. Operating on a lucid-less mind.

Indeed, life sometimes ensures that you go through your worst fear. I have had to make the trips to hell and back several times and each time into a much darker abyss until one day it was not just an abyss I had entered in the ocean, it was the hadalpelagic zone itself. I believe my mind had brought me here to kill me.

My first admission to a mental health institution seemed like a futile exercise because I was sure that this doctor that Dr Onke Tshiki had referred me to was not going to reach where I had already gone. I had already gone too far that even at the airport I had to be carried in a wheelchair because I was too weak to walk by myself or carry my luggage. I knew that I had reached the stage of palliation. However, I could not articulate this realisation to my carers. At some point, a part of me was ready to move to the other side. I loathed seeing my children watch me waste away. I remember crying throughout the admission process because I was so suicidal and had to be on a suicide watch. I wanted to die so much because this voice kept reiterating that I was useless and that my children did not need a mother like me that couldn't look after them. The two weeks in the institution felt long and it was so difficult to even join the occupational therapy sessions.

The sessions with my doctor mended the first cracks of my broken psyche. I remember meeting my psychiatrist for the very first time. It seemed so strange that he formulated a plan of helping someone who looked like me at the time, I looked like I was not alive anymore. I was emaciated because even in High School I had never reached that weight. I looked so sick and demented that I thought he was going to tell me that there was no help for me. The best thing about him is that even now he makes a plan when I suffer from severe side effects. Recently he had put me on an antidepressant that made me vomit profusely even when we switched to taking it in the night-time. Even then, he makes a plan. He sees hope and futurity when he sees me. He asks about my children, and he wants me to be the mother to them that they deserve. I am grateful for this man that I am not even related to, but he makes sure that my mental health is stable, for the times he can control it.

Many experiences happened to me whilst admitted, I would look for my mother and be so sure that these nurses have stolen her from me. I would look everywhere, in their cupboards even in the smallest spaces. As you are busy with your own psychosis someone else is busy with theirs. I remember a lady who must have gone to the kitchen a million times to try to drink some water and come back and sit down for less than a minute and go to the kitchen again. Whilst that is going on there was a beautiful Asian lady who looked my age. She said she was married once and lived with her parents who did not want her to have a life of her own. She would have these outbursts when seeing people's clothes including mine. One minute she is telling us that she was best friends with Mama Winnie, and they were in the struggle together and the next minute she is asking some random person going about their business why she is not wearing a cardigan by Chanel or any of the exclusive fashion houses. I apologised every time she hated my clothes, and I would ask her to help me look for my mother. The most beautiful thing is that although that was a tough admission with a group that had tough problems, I dreamt some weeks later that we were in an Edgars store and some of us were coming up the escalators and we all met. The first thing that I remember was that we were all whole, we spoke things that made sense. She was no longer saying she suspects she was adopted and an ANC activist that fought before 1994. We were all normal again, although that is not a term I attach much value to. Normality is a state of mind that people can use to describe how they feel at a point in time, I think there are many feelings and ways or words we can use to describe ourselves that go beyond normal. I don't think I will ever be among the normal, I want to be among the happy and the ones who know themselves and their truth. I want to be numbered always among the ones who fought hard to pursue their identity which then led to their happiness.

There are two very vivid experiences that I would like to share in this section on my worsening mental health, as mentioned before in the introduction I was lost yet I was there. It was a challenging time for the people who loved me and cared for me to watch me waste away as I was. This happened when I had just returned from the hospital but seemed worse than when I had been taken there by my family. Depression takes away your strength as if some dark magic has been performed on you. The easiest things that you never considered to be problematic suddenly become Mount Everest. My mother and her sister, my aunt Phumeza, decided to take things into their own hands. Oh, how those women raised my children without a single complaint. My aunt even came to work at the practice, and this ensured that things like the telephone and cartridges were saved because of her presence and the staff knew not to mess with her.

My mom and aunt decided that it was time to consult a traditional healer and went to inform my uncle of this decision. My uncle has a long history of not understanding their methods, but he saw the look on their faces and knew it was time to go with all of us without complaints. I understood that my mother was prepared to move heaven and earth if that was going to help me become normal again. I would hear her from my room telling my children that she wishes they had known their mother when she was her healthy normal self, suddenly this quote came to mind as I was pondering this statement she made repeatedly, "One of the hardest things you will ever have to do, my dear, is to grieve the loss of a person who is still alive."—Jeannette Walls.

Both my aunt and mom had no idea which traditional healer to consult, and they called Bhuti Mlindi, he is the man who brought the suit and shoes my ex-husband wore to his first interview in East London. He is a part of our family. Bhuti Mlindi informed us of a great male traditional healer who must have lived about an hour away from us. I did not want to have my own ideas on the matter because I was already being taken care of like a child. When we arrived at the place of this male healer we were told that he does not work on a Sunday. Luckily Bhuti Mlindi also knew about an old lady who was also good even though she was not as good as the initial person we had hoped to consult with. We travelled to this kind granny's place and luckily for us, she had not gone to church because of severe Osteoarthritis. She took us to a small house. She informed us that she will tell us, which person had come to consult without us telling her. She kept pointing at the wrong people, first my aunt, then my uncle, and then my mother, it started looking more like a joke at this point. When she was told that I was the unwell person she thought we were making a mistake.

She told us that she is going to give me products that are going to make me look even more beautiful and that beautiful people don't get sick. She gave me things to wash and moisturise with even though I don't have a problem with dry skin. She also gave me something that looked like a lucky bean and asked me to put it in my wallet. My uncle and aunt were also given so many products that they never used themselves, but I was expected to use them. Two days after seeing the kind old lady there were giant lucky beans all over my house, inside and outside. Both my mom and I were very scared as we were reminded of Jack and the Beanstalk, and we had no one to ask about what was going on. It was our secret problem. That is what happens when, in moments of desperation, we seek quick fixes and they become problems we don't know how to fix.

Anything in life that gives an instant solution without any kind of work on your part is not real. I have lost hundreds and thousands of rands looking for a quick fix in money situations and now I grieve all those monies because those people I gave monies to start by blocking me on social media and then the phone. I have learnt this the hard way. We kept praying that they would go away until one day the beans were gone.

My real problem was that I was given a generic drug instead of giving me the real drug which was on the original script. The pharmacist had erroneously forgotten to ask if I desired a generic. Sometimes with psychiatric medication, the generics do not work. I was getting worse, and I was too afraid to say to my family or my psychiatrist that I was unwell despite a recent admission. My symptoms were crippling because I did not want to look as though I was enjoying being sick. Indeed, many people supported me, and I did not want to let them down or make them tire of looking after me.

I have mentioned that I suffer from severe suicidal ideations, the tablet that works wonders for this condition for me is Lithium, but it came at a cost. It gave me such debilitating headaches that there was a time when I cut my mattress because it seemed that the headaches would improve if I slept inside a mattress. This did nothing for the headaches except ensure that the other half of the mattress would be too heavy for me. The headaches felt like they started at the hair root, and I cut off my hair, but still, they were persistent. Then even the scalp felt like the origin, and I got tired of trying my remedies and consulted with my psychiatrist. He stopped the Lithium and after a few months, he started me on a drug called Epitec. He cautioned me that if I developed a rash I must stop it immediately.

About a week or two after I had started the treatment I noticed red dots on my legs and stopped the treatment. The dots only went further up my body and changed their morphology from red dots to a full-on rash. Just as that was starting I bled, from the mouth, the vagina, and the rectum, every orifice. I was diagnosed with Steven Johnson Syndrome which needed some steroids that are administered in ICU. I was surrounded by my family and doctors and decided on getting comfort care. I had never seen someone live and beat Steven Johnson Syndrome and I did not expect to be the first person I knew who could beat it. Therefore, I chose to be taken care of at home till my time comes.

Long before hospitals became abundant, the process of death took place in the home. I would not choose to be surrounded by alarms and phlebotomists taking my blood in the pursuit of determining what was wrong with me. In other words, I will never choose rigorous methods to preserve my life, even though I have children. I love them and they know that. They know every decision I have ever made before I even had them were steps that were made in love, for them. I choose peace at the end of my life; in this case, I had a physiotherapist who did not give up even though my entire skin removed itself and I lost the ability to walk. We would still do exercises and I would scream in agony every time he touched me. My mom once decided to join one of the sessions, she could not watch me go through the pain, but once it was over I could watch my children swim through the window. I was not the mom who went to the hospital and never came back, I was the mom who chose to be present till the end. I would love them till the end.

I even played chess with them and would move my pieces by telling them the names of the squares. Mom was very sick, mom could die, but mom was home and they understood that mom chose them. That made them strong, they were not afraid to look at me, to tell me how much they loved me. I was happy that we went through this tough time as a family, it was a lesson that families remain intact forever. That whether I was here or on the other side, I was their mother and would be till the end of time.

I had never envisaged that I would go through with making palliative decisions in my thirties. I think everyone in their thirties is looking forward to living and working very hard to make it the one they have dreamt of. Here I was in the palliative stage of my life which meant that I had accepted another fate, that of pain control and being at home instead of the more aggressive treatments that are done in the hospital but sometimes have no real successes. If that was the case then everyone who went to the hospital would come out healed. That is not always the case now, is it?

I wish people realised that their fate does not have to be tied to a hospital that they have the autonomy to choose to stay at home when they reach diagnoses that cannot be solved by modern medicine. That even their families realise that dying with dignity in your own home is not the worst thing to happen to you versus taking end-stage renal failure or cancer patients who are in palliative stages to the casualty department at night where they are seen by overworked doctors who have no idea why they are there. We must change the current narrative, the fact that we are mortal is a truth that will never change. How we deal with the decisions surrounding our mortality and its end is up to us. May we make the right decisions that honour, not only our lives but teach generations about what it means to be mortal. There is a book authored by Atul Gawande called *Being Mortal*. Here are some words to share on his opinions and research on this matter, "Our ultimate goal, after all, is not a good death but a good life to the very end". My story became one of triumph, I recovered, and my skin started its restoration process. These are the things we continue to lose in the blazing flames that represent the fire in our lives, in my case this was the story of the worst drug reaction I have suffered so far.

I would need three more admissions and a myriad of diagnoses before I could return to something even remotely similar to who I used to be. Returning to who I used to be was the reason for putting up such a fight, even though it was the longest fight of my life. I thought that it would be possible in the future to not use sleeping tablets, but now I think that I will use them for the rest of my life alongside Lithium which takes away all the suicidal ideations to which I am prone.

My psychologist said something powerful, she encouraged me to improve on the version of me I already was and stop chasing a ghost who is a much younger and less experienced version of myself. This worked. I was able to look back on the things that had broken me and caused me to have such a fragile mind. I was able to make sense of many decisions and yet it would take years before

I was able to identify some aspects of myself that were starting to return. I firmly believe that when my mother chose to die, she decided to die and leave me her strength instead because I have never been as strong as when my mother died. It has taken many years to repair my self-esteem, deflated self-concept, deflated self-worth, worsening self-distrust, self-doubt, and deeply rooted auto criticism.

I have even learnt the virtue of what lies in being gentle with oneself. May you learn this important lesson and read the full text of Desiderata.

Desiderata
By Max Ehrmann[15]

Go placidly amid the noise and the haste, and remember what peace there may be in silence. As far as possible, without surrender, be on good terms with all persons. Speak your truth quietly and clearly; and listen to others, even to the dull and the ignorant; they too have their story. Avoid loud and aggressive persons; they are vexatious to the spirit.

If you compare yourself with others, you may become vain or bitter, for always there will be greater and lesser persons than yourself. Enjoy your achievements as well as your plans. Keep interested in your own career, however humble; it is a real possession in the changing fortunes of time.

Exercise caution in your business affairs, for the world is full of trickery. But let this not blind you to what virtue there is; many persons strive for high ideals, and everywhere life is full of heroism. Be yourself. Especially do not feign affection. Neither be cynical about love; for in the face of all aridity and disenchantment, it is as perennial as the grass. Take kindly the counsel of the years, gracefully surrendering the things of youth. Nurture strength of spirit to shield you in sudden misfortune. But do not distress yourself with dark imaginings. Many fears are born of fatigue and loneliness. Beyond a wholesome discipline, be gentle with yourself. You are a child of the universe no less than the trees and the stars; you have a right to be here. And whether or not it is clear to you, no doubt the universe is unfolding as it should.

Therefore, be at peace with God, whatever you conceive Him to be. And whatever your labors and aspirations, in the noisy confusion of life, keep peace in your soul. With all its sham, drudgery and broken dreams, it is still a beautiful world. Be cheerful.
Strive to be happy.

HOW IT MAY HAVE STARTED

SINKING OF THE MENDI
By S.E.K. Mqhayi16

UKUTSHONA KUKAMENDI

Ewe, le nto kakade yinto yaloo nto.
Thina, nto zaziyo, asothukanga nto;
Sibona kamhlope, sithi bekumelwe,
Sitheth'engqondweni, sithi kufanelwe;
Xa bekungenjalo bekungayi kulunga.
Ngoko ke, Sotase! Kwaqal'ukulunga!
Le nqanaw', umendi, namhla yendisile,
Na'igazi lethu lisikhonzisile!

Asinithenganga ngazo izicengo;
Asinithenganga ngayo imibengo;
Bekungenganzuzo zimakhwesikhwezi,
Bekungenganzuzo ingangeenkwenkwezi.
Sikwatsho nakuni, bafel'eAfrika,
KwelaseJamani yaseMpumalanga,
NelaseJamani yaseNtshonalanga.
Bekungembek'eninayo kuKumkani,
Bekungentobeko yenu kwiBritani.

It Can Turn

Mhla nashiy' ikhaya sithethile nani,
Mhla nashiy'iintsaposalathile kuni,
Mhla sabamb'izandla, mhla kwamanz'amehlo.
Mhla balil'oonyoko, bangqukrulek'ooyihlo,
Mhla nazishiy'ezi ntaba zakowenu,
Nayinikel'imiv'imilmb'ezwe lenu
Ayitshongo na kuni, midak' akowethu,
Ukuthi "Kwelo zwe nilidini lethu?"

Ngesibinge ngantonina ke kade?
Idini lomzi liyintonina ke kade?
Asingamathol'amaduna omzina?
Asizizithandwa zesizwe kade na?
Ngoku kuthethe ke siyendelisela,
Sibhekis'ezantsi, sihlahla indlela.
AsinguHabheli na idini lomhlaba?
AsinguMesiya na elasezulwini?

Thuthuzelekani ngoko, zinkedama!
Thuthuzelekani ngoko, bafazana!
Kuf'omnye kade mini kwakhiw' omnye;
Kukhonza mnye kade' ze kuphil' abanye;
Ngala mazwi sithi, thuthuzelekani,
Ngokwenjenje kwethu sithi, yakhekani.
Lithatheni eli qhalo labadala,
Kuba bathi: "Akuhlanga lungehlanga!

Awu! Zaf'int'ezinkulu zeAfrika!
Isindiwe le nqanawa, 'de yazika,
Kwf'amakhalipha, amafa nankosi,
Agazi lithetha kwiNkosi yeeNkosi.
Ukufa kwawo kunomvuzo nomvuka
Ndinga ndingema nawo ngomhla wovuko,
Ndingqambe njengomnye osebenzileyo,
Ndikhanye njengomso oqaqambileyo.
Makube njalo!

SINKING OF THE MENDI

Yes, this thing flows as a normal thing from that.
The thing we know is not scared of that;
We say, things have happened as they should have,
Within our brains we say: it should have been so;
If it hadn't been so, nothing would have come right.
You see Sotase, things came right when the Mendi sank!
Our blood on that ship turned things around,
It served to make us known through the world!

The British didn't buy us with begging;
They didn't seduce us with long strips of meat;
They didn't bribe us with things as high as the stars,
They didn't bribe us with profits.
We say unto those who died, you were Africans,
Those who died in the country of the rising sun,

161

It Can Turn

Those who died in the country of the setting sun,
You didn't die out of subservience for the king,
Nor because you wanted to kowtow to Britain.

On the day you left home, we talked,
On the day you left, we promised to look after your families,
On this day we shook hands, our eyes were wet.
On this day mothers cried, your fathers sobbed,
On this day you left the mountains of your birth,
You left the rivers of our country behind
We said to you, going there as dark-skinned men,
We said: "You are our sacrifice from here."

Could we have sacrificed anything more precious?
What did it mean to sacrifice a village?
Was it not giving the bull calves of your homestead?
Sending those very ones who loved you as a nation?
We're talking deep now; we have added our voice,
Proudly we are part of those opening the road to freedom.
In the way Abel was the sacrifice of the earth?
In the way the Messiah was the sacrifice of heaven?

Be consoled, all you orphans!
Be consoled, all you young widows!
Somebody has to die, so that something can be built;
Somebody has to serve, so that others can live;
With these words we say: be consoled,
This is how we build ourselves, as ourselves.

Remember the saying of the old people:
"Nothing comes down, without coming down."

Awu! The finest of Africa was busy dying!
The ship couldn't carry its precious cargo,
It was echoing into the inner circles,
Their brave blood faced the King of Kings.
Their deaths had a purpose for all of us
How I wish I could be with them,
How I wish I could stand with them on resurrection day,
How I wish I could sparkle with them like the morning star.
Let it be so!

The above poem, as long as it is, was the perfect example of what I understood a catastrophe to be. We were taught at school about the sacrifices that these men made for a country that meant nothing to them only to meet death in foreign waters. I always cried when I read it. We read it in our Xhosa language, and I hope it is still being taught because it is our history. When I think about the worst thing that happened to me and how it may have started, I remember these men first. The fracturing and breakage of my mind must have started after my beautiful cousin Nombuyiselo died. Her night-time visitations made its effects seem less intense, but there was a hole in my life that could not be filled or repaired as in many structural defects of the heart in infants and children. This was not a ventricular or atrial septal defect with an exact size with a definite treatment plan nor a coarctation of the aorta or Tetralogy of Fallot. This was far more complex—this was my life. For the first time, I had been met with a challenge that I could not reverse. Death is unalterable, it remains the same, permanent.

My young and growing mind could not grasp these issues of impermanence, loss, and the value or virtue that lies in letting go. It would take years to master these seemingly simple principles. It took years to find the meaning her death deserved, I simply chose to grieve for the longest time. I am not sure if it was a choice more than a condition I had to live with. I grieved and grieved till I thought it would also consume me.

The church council may have been designed to be a tool to assist in my restoration and repentance process, however, it did the opposite, it changed me. It forever changed the little neurons in my mind that found safety and goodness in men. I grew up without a father as he had ended his life. These were my surrogate fathers. They destroyed whatever trust I would have in the future for the male species and destroyed whatever emotional or psychological patterns that are related to men. Even years of therapy have not been able to bring back the years lost after that one fateful day where I experienced hell on earth in the most literal sense of the word. I am no longer afraid of hell, I have met monsters who will reside in that realm with me, their victim. The sexual assaults that they instigated against my fragile mind remain, the main trigger for my pandora's box to open.

My mental health was *guarded and hangs in doubt*, a term used during ward rounds when discussing the prognoses of patients in hospitals. When a prognosis is guarded it is uncertain and as doctors, we start to worry for the patient and their family as we have no concrete answers.

A beautiful long-time friend recently said, "Zikhona, I have not watched you experience any real closure with this issue, and I suggest that since it has now been more than two decades that you do something about it." She also thanked me for sharing my experience with her because she was forewarned about what one could go through in the repentance process. It must be understood that no one forced me to go to the Bishop, I did it out of respect for the body which I believed and had been taught was a temple. I did it out of respect for the principle and saving ordinance of repentance. I did it out of my love and admiration for Joseph Smith.

The best way that I can explain my very rapid mental decline would be this, it comes like a thief into the night. Can you imagine how things were on 7 December 1941 just before 8:00 a.m., when Japan attacked an unknowing and unprepared America that had tried so hard to be neutral throughout World War Two, even though it had its allies? One day I was a successful doctor who had so much to live for, a booming practice that could only be described in miraculous ways. The next moment I was a drifter with no real anchor. I had forgotten where I needed to go. I tried to be the person I knew myself to be, but she was gone. Too many traumas had occurred following my blissful childhood—the days of climbing trees and stealing peaches were gone forever. I could not get her back no matter how hard I tried.

A progressively fracturing mind does not come shouting and yelling bearing gifts, it is silent and takes whatever it wants. It starts with a feeling of yearning to sleep forever. I would sleep for days at a time and the walk to the bathroom felt like a walk to Mount Everest without any oxygen or appropriate gear to secure me. For a while, it seemed as though nappies would do a quicker job and they became a saviour. Bathing was a situation that just was not part of my day. I did not even smell myself; I also did not care. I survived on sleeping pills, when I woke up I took more to send me to another stupor of sleep and the vicious cycle carried on for months. My mother tried to wake me up and feed me even once a day, but it was difficult. I was so depressed and wanted to die and begged her to allow me to die but she kept begging me to stay. I was flurrying.

This rapid mental decline does everything that will benefit its cause of reducing you to nothing. Mystery dust of nothingness envelopes you, this carries on for so long that it becomes your new life. It has no regard for what it does to your children. It leaves nothing for them even though they must know that they need you. They are young and this is a confusing time for them and only the love and support of a mother will suffice, but it leaves nothing for them. It left my children with a mother they could not recognise. Even the quality of my voice changed. I could not recognise the sound of my voice. It took everything from me, like a house that had been burgled and only its shell stood and unmovable objects like rocks remained. My unmovable objects quickly turned into diagnoses, tablets, mental health institution admissions, more tablets, weight gain, worsening self-esteem, patients asking where I've been and when I would return. I continue to battle to answer all these questions.

I have never been able to work full-time since my divorce, and diagnoses for depression, generalised anxiety disorder, and bipolar type 2. I have gone through many unpalatable demented, depressive, and psychotic encounters in my forty years of life and still none compares to being beaten by a white geriatric lady who had confused me for a white person for some time because of my pale skin and when she found out I was black I was deserving of a beating. The nurses gave me Panado. The experiences you bear witness to in a mental institution are precious and eye-opening, they make you look at yourself with a different kind of lens.

I remember arriving and realising that a bed was not booked for me. The alternative was sleeping in the male side of the hospital. I guarded myself that whole night. I was looking out the window from night until dawn. I had such a deep-rooted mistrust and scarring when it came to men. My demented suicidal mind never made the connection that I could have gone to sleep by the nurses' station. I remember this admission very well because it brought to the surface something that I had locked in my subconscious.

I shared a story with my psychiatrist about the horror of the night before and my trauma with having to sleep near men. My conscious mind had not recalled that something deeply disturbing had occurred to me two months before this admission. I had buried it so deep because I feared the mayhem and disarray that acknowledging it would bring to my already fragile self. What I was able to tell my psychiatrist was this: I had an appointment towards the end of 2008 with a physiotherapist who wanted to rent a room in my practice to see patients. He would be booked twice a week. He was a young and well-mannered man and I wanted to give him a chance. He had left public practice and was struggling to make it on his own, as all of us did when we started. We ended up engaging on many topics and did not realise that the mall we had had lunch at was closing because it was a Sunday.

The restaurant was still open thus our inability to notice the time. Having children alienates you a little from other adult interactions which is why this was a captivating experience for me. Hearing innovative ideas from someone so much younger than me was enthralling. When the lunch was over we then went our separate ways to our cars. Unfortunately, we parked on opposite sides of the parking lot which had been deserted. As I approached my car, I noticed a black Polo directly opposite my car and two men seemed to be chilling and enjoying themselves; I greeted them, and I continued towards my car. The second man started pursuing me and I started to run in uncomfortable stilettos as I was scared for my life. He had his hands behind his back and asked if I thought I was the only woman on earth who had refused advances from a man. I politely asked him to show his hands as a dead woman's body was found in the same mall a month before this incident.

His hands were empty, and I proceeded to my car and erroneously clicked the button on my remote twice (which unlocked the car). He was in my car as soon as I had also entered and at that moment, I was his girlfriend. I just remember that his skin was extremely dark—the darkest I had ever experienced a person to be. He performed an onslaught of a sexual offence that I was unable to stop. During the entire ordeal, he kept threatening me by saying that if I ever told his wife about our affair, he would murder me. He kept repeating that he had a good marriage and did not need complications like me hindering his happiness. What did not make sense to me was that I did not even know his name, how then would I know his wife? After he had completed his dreadful acts on me, he ordered me to drive to my house or flat or wherever I lived. Once we left the mall, I planned to flee as soon as I came across the first set of traffic lights.

He asked where I lived, and I lied and said I lived in the Mdantsane township. He was so disgusted by my answer that he asked me to stop the car and suddenly he vanished. Like Aslan, there was no trace of him, and I drove straight home. I was thirty-eight years old and felt too embarrassed to go to the police station to report a rape. I was scared that I would be taken to a hospital where the doctor who will be explaining and performing the procedure would be someone I had either worked with or someone I knew. This reminded me of when I had to take a sexually transmitted disease profile when I was known by everyone at the lab to be a married woman. I sobbed the whole time.

My mom said it was okay for me to choose to not follow the path of going to the police and instead come home for comfort and safety. She was very empathetic and saddened by the events that had occurred and I knew that she knew that I would end up in a hospital bed, not in a courtroom like other rape survivors. My psychiatrist helped me work on my healing and getting past the experience that I could not change. I felt that too much time had passed for me to even open a police file as I had nothing—no name, no DNA evidence in case it could be matched with other unsolved similar crimes or even fingerprints.

I have profound guilt for not going through the process of the law as it may have saved another woman. It did not seem like the right path for me at that time. I have thought about this on many occasions and realised that there were many red flags that I ignored before the onslaught. When I noticed that there were no other cars in the parking lot, I could have gone to find security guards, employed by the mall, to escort me to my car. Also, for the longest time, I blamed myself for this situation over the fact that I clicked the remote twice, but I later realised that a person who had his mind fixed on destroying a stranger's life would have found other means to disempower me.

The true message is this: as women, we are not safe, not even in a mall. People who have a propensity to cause harm, do not lurk silently in dark alleys; they are among us. It falls on us to be vigilant at all costs. There are too many stories shared daily of such attacks and I now add my story to the ones already shared by different victims. I am a victim of rape and I still pursue my dreams, no matter what the cost. He has not taken my spirit to fight for my completeness, wholeness, and my beautiful ability to dream.

Unlike some of my friends, I have been lucky enough to have had all my admissions voluntarily and got the help I needed from the scourge of suicidal thoughts and obsession with death. My friends who are also mental healthcare users always say I am lucky because their admissions involved the police and involuntary admissions. We laugh over these just as we cry when one of us has developed kidney failure due to lithium toxicity. I depend on lithium for my life, and I count how many years before I reach that same fate too. I will know though that when the time comes, lithium offered me a solution no other tablet could—an end to debilitating suicidal ideations. I will be forever grateful for that relief.

There are two kinds of suicidal ideations, passive and active. Passive suicidal ideation usually relates to wishing that you were dead or that you could die without any set plans to carry out the suicide. Active suicidal ideations are far more complex. In this instance, these are not just thoughts of suicide but there is an intent that includes concrete plans to accomplish this. In my experiences of interacting with adult children whose parents had taken their own lives, it became evident that most of their parents had started with parasuicides, the acts of attempting to kill yourself but not achieving any success in doing it. They had been trying to kill themselves as far back as teenagerhood. This information was kept a secret from their children by the parents. This seemed like a huge betrayal from their grandparents as the knowledge could have prepared them in their perspective.

Suicidal ideation is one of the symptoms of both major depression and the depression found in bipolar disorder, but it can be found in an entire range of mental illnesses. The American poet Sylvia Plath who suffered from severe depression describes suicidal ideation in raw and graphic detail when she wrote the following: "Dying is an art, like everything else. I do it exceptionally well. I do it so it feels like hell. I do it so it feels real. I guess you could say I've a call." Unfortunately, Plath completed her suicide on 11 February 1963 by sticking her head in an oven after many previous attempts which date back to August 1953. She was 30 years old, and sadly her son also succumbed to the same fate in March 2009, also after a lifelong battle with depression.

The lifetime prevalence of suicidal ideation for the general world population is about 9% and about 2% within twelve months. These numbers are different for people with mental health disorders. The exact numbers remain elusive and since ideation is a symptom of many mental health disorders, the exact prevalence is not readily measurable.

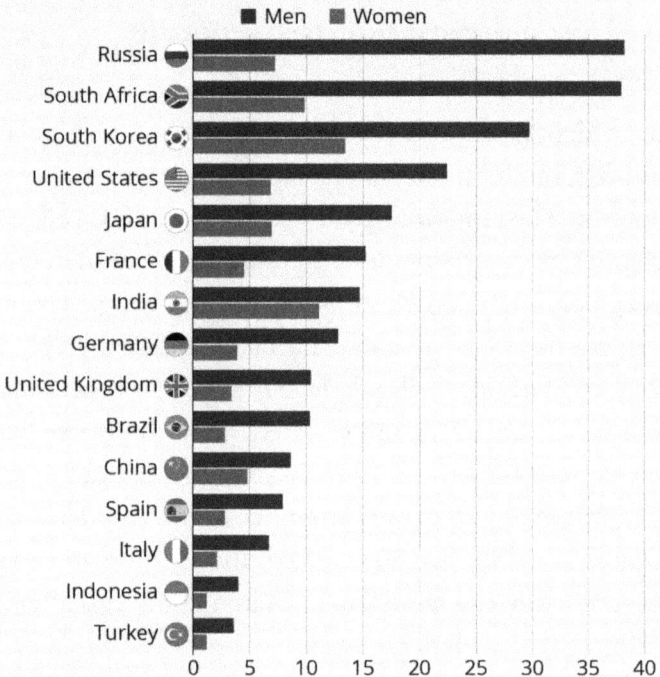

Suicide Rates Around the World

Estimated rate of suicide per 100,000 population in selected countries in 2019

■ Men ■ Women

Country	Men	Women
Russia	38	7
South Africa	37.5	9.5
South Korea	30	13
United States	22	6
Japan	17.5	7
France	15	4.5
India	14.5	11
Germany	12.5	4
United Kingdom	10	3
Brazil	10	2.5
China	8.5	5
Spain	7.5	2.5
Italy	6.5	2
Indonesia	4	1
Turkey	3.5	1

Source: WHO

statista

Suicide Rates Around the World from statista.com

There was a very difficult time when the suicidal ideations were not lifting, and an urgent meeting was called with the trustees of my trust. One of them Hlombe, a trusted confidant and loyal beautiful friend since the first day of the Bachelor of Science in Dietetics degree. She shared a very touching and endearing story which I will relay in the way it was intended for when this enemy of suicidal ideations and thoughts attacks. She shared that she had a dream a few years ago where she was in this decrepit taxi—which seemed odd since she has had a car for decades. She overheard a conversation that was happening in the chair behind her. She had the impression that a very sweet persuasive guy was talking to a girl and trying to get her affections and her phone number. She was trying hard not to listen to the conversation, but they were loud, and the guy was so impressive and old-fashioned in his approach to the girl. She was taken aback by his authenticity and the degree he demonstrated his willingness to be with her, in a taxi ride of all things! He sounded perfectly innocent. When the taxi came to a standstill, the lady turned to him and asked for his name, he said my name is Suicide. Immediately it made the greatest sense to me: when the suicidal ideations or thoughts arrive, they are not harsh or shouting, they simply bargain with you as they affirm things you already know about yourself, your low self-esteem, your inadequateness as a mother, as a doctor, as a citizen. How much happier everyone would be without you.

Mental disorders are real. They can be genetic; some are shared, and this means you start to present the same symptoms as the mental healthcare user that you are looking after. Many mental health advocates have risen in the past few years, and this has been marvellous, as there are voices that speak on our behalf and that have made us rise and have the courage to speak about our afflictions. We thank you for your witness, for standing next to us over an illness that is so universally misunderstood, an illness most people have not suffered from.

We must disclose when initiating new policies, especially life policies, and we are declined, I suppose because of the suicidal ideation aspect of our illness and our boundless and incessant state of painfully constant affairs. In fact, even planning what we are going to embark on just the following day is a lot for us. We must take each day gracefully and always remember to be kind to ourselves first. In Don Miguel Ruiz's book, *The four agreements*, we are taken on a beautiful ride of self-love, self-affirmations, wisdom, and putting boundaries between unrealistic expectations and ourselves. The first agreement says, 'Be impeccable with your word.' This is a truth I am attempting to live by even with my children. A lot of confusion is circumvented by just being impeccable with your word. We thank mankind for lending an ear to an illness that might not necessarily involve you but still, you stand for our suffering. You read the books and understand the very special lives we lead. We are grateful for the help received through our mental healthcare practitioners, for assisting us to find bits and pieces of meaning, completeness, wholeness, and some degrees of functionality.

CHAPTER 6:

THE ART OF GRIEF

"No one ever told me that grief felt so like fear. I am not afraid, but the sensation is like being afraid. The same fluttering in the stomach, the same restlessness, the yawning. I keep on swallowing."
—C. S. Lewis from A Grief Observed

As a young adult, I came across the five stages of grief written by Elizabeth Kübler-Ross in 1969, a psychiatrist who observed dying or terminally ill people. Her findings brought about the conclusions that we are all familiar with, denial, anger, bargaining, depression, and acceptance. It must also be acknowledged that there are criticisms of her work and so it is okay if none of these stages is relatable to you. Not everyone will experience grief, despite going through a severely life-changing experience. We are mentally, biologically, physically, psychologically different in our life experiences.

Denial: Due to the overwhelming nature of grief, it is natural for denial of the event to set in. This could be a loss of employment, loss of marriage, or loss of a loved one. Denial is the body's natural defence system against this gigantic mountain ahead of you and for a while it allows you to cope. The end of this stage is marked by an acknowledgement that this has indeed happened. All the feelings are now brought to the surface. In the context of a marriage ending, denial comes before the divorce. The divorce itself is the result of not being able to lie to yourself anymore. I was in denial; my mind did not want to see my marriage for what it truly was. The protection this stage provides is that it buys you time. It tells you the blood results given to you by your doctor on a very grave diagnosis may have belonged to someone else and more tests will vilify the diagnosis. It tells you that a dead person is not really dead, how can they be if you can still hear their voice in your ear?

Anger: This phase is more marked by frustration, irritation, and extremes of anxiety and agitation. This is when blame sets in, and the anger gets redirected to the people who did not cause it. A lot of questions form part of this stage including beliefs about the existence of a God. Why have you been chosen to suffer? Why has this calamity chosen your home now instead of next door because the people next door might be stronger? In my case, I never really wanted to date a younger man, but my family convinced me that he was legit, and I was angry. I was angry that the decision to be with him was not entirely my decision and I bought into his musings. He would even tell me lines from movies that he must have thought I had not seen. I was angry that I did not see through him.

Bargaining: During this stage, people often beg and make deals with God or whoever their source of light and truth is. "If my husband survives being ventilated following this COVID-19 pandemic, then I will be a better mother and wife." The main characteristics of this stage are desperation and regrets because sadly, the glass has already been broken into a million little pieces. Nothing can be done at his stage. Even if people use this tool to try to get back together in marriages, lasting happiness is not guaranteed. We sometimes bargain our way out of accepting and dealing with our reality.

Depression: For me, depression came in many forms. The pain I felt was extraordinary, it was something that I had never experienced before, nor would I ever allow myself to feel again. Every fibre of my being was in turmoil. My cells were screaming at the thought of a life changed forever. They were at war with each other and each laid blame on the other for not seeing and signalling that a battle was on its way. All they did all day was scream in agony. My mitochondria simply decided to take a break from this chaos and madness thus the immense fatigue. My heart, my poor heart did not want to beat, it simply performed this enormous task as servitude to me, its master. It carried the task as servitude to my four beautiful children and this in turn aged it. If my heart were to be examined through various technological devices that study hearts, I believe they would all conclude that my heart was that of a hundred-year-old lady. Indeed, I have lived a hundred years, yet my chronological age is only forty years old.

This stage is the first stage that acknowledges our new reality. Grief and pain are felt most intensely. Somatic symptoms of not getting out of bed, and feeling physical pain, visceral pain that cannot be treated is also common. This pain is so intense, and it truly is mere depression. There is a withdrawal from the things that previously mattered to you. There is a sense of wanting to be alone, and the hopelessness can lead to suicidal thoughts. It is a very difficult stage.

Acceptance: In this stage, there is a sense of understanding and owning the loss and its reality. The reality may be complex, intricate, and life-altering but it is acknowledged anyway. The depression and suicidal ideations may lift and there is an understanding that life is forever changed but life is not dead. A common saying in the religion of the Drowned God on the Iron Islands in the Game of Thrones is that what is dead may never die. I interpret it to mean that as you begin the work of acceptance you cannot die again. Grief needs to be dealt with delicately, fully, so that you do not continue to die forever.

I don't know when I stopped thinking about my husband or when I may have stopped loving him or stopped analysing why things became what they became. I accepted that I was not a perfect wife. I thought everything I did was for the betterment of our family life, but I suspect more was needed from me. I have let all that go. I think the people of the Mormon church needed a young girl to ask sexual questions to. It was an experiment, and they had no idea how destructive and traumatic it would become. They never considered that life would be lost in that makeshift courtroom. It was meant for people like me with no voice, no parents in the church. The courts will decide how this matter is closed, not just for the child I used to be, but for all children that are exploited by men in powerful positions just because they can, it can be a church, school, even in your own home.

I have gone through these stages countless times as I processed the deaths and losses of my father and the death of my beloved cousin, my marriage, my abuse by the Mormon church, and the death of my mother. They come in no set order, but they come.

THE SIXTH STAGE OF GRIEF

A new book explaining the sixth stage of grief has blown my mind. David Kessler writes that the sixth stage of grief is, *finding meaning*. Meaning is all around us, but it is that one ingredient that allows you to look at life in a different light. My father committed suicide at the age of twenty-four, thus rendering me fatherless. I have thought often about what factors must prevail for one to decide that life is no longer needed. I've gone to his grave, interviewed his friends, and spoken to him in my mind to find out what may have led him to take his life. From what I can decipher after all those conversations, I know my father never wanted to leave me. I know that whatever drove him to that must have been an illness, a mental illness.

It took a very long time for mental illnesses to receive the kind of recognition and treatment they so rightfully deserved and as a result his father, my grandfather had also succumbed to the same fate—he had also taken his life. The bigger question which now remains, which will always remain is this, as their DNA courses through my veins, what genes have they left behind? Am I also going to succumb to the same fate, or will I be protected by the gods, by God, by the unequivocal love I have for my children?

I have found comfort in knowing that all the people who have left me never did it by choice. Through finding meaning, I have found a greater strength within me. I have been able, under these circumstances of death, to keep growing, to keep moving, to keep striving, seeking and to never yield as Alfred Lord Tennyson wrote in Ulysses.

THE TRUTH OF GRIEF

"Everything that lives must die. But while life has to end, love doesn't."
—David Kessler

Grief is toxic. It has no good intentions than to watch you wither away and become a shadow of your former self. I once asked my psychologist why I was not becoming me again after all these years of therapy. This is because when grief changes us, we are aware that our essence is changing, and this becomes a conundrum for us. She asked me why I would want to go back to the past instead of embracing this new me with all my new possibilities. I was taken aback because I truly believed therapy was about taking all my trillion little pieces and putting them back together again so that I can be whole again. Little did I know that I had to work with the raw ingredients in front of me and mould them into a workable version of myself that I have grown to love because of the resilience that it possesses.

I admire the strength built through these losses and pain. It has made me wiser and has brought meaning to my life. I no longer see a foreign person in the mirror, I see me. Ours is to face grief, deal with it, make sense of it and as we find the meaning of our grief, find the strength to also put it away.

This search for meaning will be unique for all of us, like how we perceive life. We view it to be difficult and easier for other people. Sometimes other people follow a path that looks so easy from the person watching and other lives look so complex that you even thank your gods or lucky stars for not being given that life. It is the same with meaning. Searching for meaning will lead us all in different directions but what is important is to find it at the end of your odyssey. It will seem ridiculously easy for others whilst it remains incredibly difficult for those of us like me. That's why life will always be mythological, we are not born the same way.

CONCLUSION

Thanatopsis
By William Cullen Bryant[17]

"So live, that when thy summons comes to join
The innumerable caravan, which moves
To that mysterious realm, where each shall take
His chamber in the silent halls of death,
Though go not, like the quarry-slave at night,
Scourged to his dungeon, but, sustained and soothed
By an unfaltering trust, approach thy grave,
Like one who wraps the drapery of his couch
About him, and lies down to pleasant dreams."

The above poem was written by a wise seventeen-year-old poet with an enduring profoundness, and it is the last part of a long and insightful poem. It implores us to live. Live such that we will have no regrets. This reminds me of an Indian Proverb that says, "he who dreams for too long will become like his shadow." We are further reminded that there is no hand to catch time.

This book is a testimony of the beauty and transitory nature of life. While its main themes are those of self-identity, finding your truth, loss, impermanence, the ability to still find meaning in your life, the courage to let go and pursue your dreams at all costs. The pursuit of one's dreams is usually met with a paralysing fear which encourages you to stop dreaming and continue a complacent and mediocre life. A journey that copies others' safe lives, never living your dreams. This is when you will need to press on the most and draw on courage, persistence, and resilience. Learning and challenging yourself through dreams that scare even you—that's when you grow.

You will be okay. I can assure you that I have gone through challenges and dreams that people have laughed about. I have had seasons of plenty, and I have had nothing at all. I have lost so many earthly possessions and people I have loved. I have no guarantees that I will not lose again, yet I fight on, with a renewed faith and quietly listen for meaning behind my grief.

No one believed that I could be a doctor with my township background. It seemed like an unrealistic dream because high school was very tough. I then started my practice without a cent in my pocket and this practice thrived and allowed for me and my children to see the world. Don't stop believing in yourself and the power of your resilient mind and resilient muscles.

I went through hell and back a million times through mental struggles that must have been triggered by the unexpected turn of events regarding the end of my marriage. The process of rebuilding whatever little pieces constituted my life was arduous and daunting. The strenuous effort of reincarnating a life for myself was not only the hardest thing I had ever done but also the most painful because in my heart of hearts I still longed for the old life. It was easier than having to start from nothing. There was a beckoning to go back to what was familiar, yet I chose to fight.

I chose to start a new life even though I was not sure if a thirty-five-year-old with four children could. I am still grateful that I experienced love, no matter how long it lasted. I now stand stronger than before because my mother left me her strength, her powers, but not her magical cooking skills. She is always nearby.

I dreamt of authoring a book and feared so many things, yet I wrote it anyway. I thought I did not have the time to write and did not believe that the message I wanted to impart would have the power to change lives or become an influence for the better. I doubted whether I had the skill since I am a Scientist, a medical doctor. I use the power of resilience to be more than I envision myself and I challenge myself as I know that I am closer to the end of my life than its beginning and would rather take chances because, within my tumultuous storms, I met me.

Throughout the book, I have used examples from my life in its parts. The volcanoes that have erupted in my psyche and delicate body have made me very vulnerable as a person. I have covered many of my life's themes with deep honesty and the resolutions and acceptances of the cards that I have been dealt. Letting go of all that no longer serves you is paramount. It emphasises that which Elizabeth Bishop taught us in a poem that was discussed earlier called, 'One Art', where she had not only lost her mother's watch, but also three loved houses, two rivers and a continent. She went through all those losses, but concluded that they were not disasters, were not catastrophes, were not life-defining possessions or did not cause calamities and ruin in her life. I read the last verse with intention every time, without breathing as I consider its reverence. I read this poem often as I like to be reminded that all these things we dream and work towards can be lost in minutes. Again, the magical word impermanence reminds us not to hold on too tightly to material things, to loved ones. Yes, love them but know that we are all offered 100% mortality and that people are fallible. They can disappoint us, even the people we make vows with, vows do not offer a 100% success rate.

Even the churches and all the religions which we rely on to define us, all come short. Time is short and very precious. It is the only commodity that we possess to enable us to be the dream-pursuing-giants that we long to be.

I want us to do this small exercise in honour of the people that we loved but that we lost through the pandemic caused by COVID-19. I will use my beautiful mother as my example. We will be inserting the names of the people we have lost in the last stanza of the poem *One Art*. Write their names with a pencil.

'Even losing you, *Ncumisa Hlalempini* (the joking voice, a gesture I love) I shan't have lied. It's evident the art of losing's not too hard to master though it may look like (Write it) like a disaster.'

My mother's life and death make more sense when I read the last stanza like this. This poem brings me to one conclusion, that you can lose it all, but the trick lies in not losing yourself in the process. I have also oftentimes lost it all and because I had no real insight, I had no hope of restoration. I only wish I had understood these truths much earlier in my life. So many things would have turned out differently. I would not have married the person my mother liked but rather a person of my choice.

She had no gun to my head. Eventually, I fell in love but if I had not gone even on a single date with him, then I would have never known such pain. That's the purpose of the book that you, the reader, become so wise that whenever I meet you, you will tell me how well you are doing, how much joy you've found in finding yourself. You must brag to me that you are living a life wiser and better informed than mine. I want you to be proud of all the decisions you make, big or small. This book was written with you in mind.

This book emphasises the resounding truth that life can only be lived once one has established their identity. The truths that define them and letting go of the things that hinder that path. Finding your identity and truth is not a straightforward process as the world is filled with so much noise. The noise can be physical as you step outside and hear the buzzing of cars and shouting of people, it can also be found within the technological devices, the illness of a loved one, financial constraints, marital challenges, opinions, expectations, and obligations, etc. In an era when you are constantly receiving notifications from emails and all other social media, it is difficult to filter that noise and if you are not consciously aware of it. You may sadly live the rest of your life without finding this identity we refer to in this book.

Start by taking time just for yourself, it could be thirty minutes a day and in this space, you re-evaluate where it is you had intended to be and how far you are from this goal. Examine, in true dissection form, why it is taking longer for you to reach where you wanted to go. Within this self-analysis, define who you are, define your truths, and define the things you will never settle for in the pursuit of yourself and your life's dreams. I write the last line purposefully for young women because if they have not worked on themselves and what their boundaries are, they could become sexual prey to old married men when seeking things like employment and funding or even love. Establishing boundaries is one of the key points in determining the value of self-worth which is a major ingredient when one is finding an identity.

Another valuable tool one can practice during these thirty minutes is meditation. I was taught many distinct types during my admissions but one that still speaks to me is this one: you need to lie on the floor and have a couch to place your legs at an almost 90-degree angle to the couch. You can have music or not but all you do is breathe. You breathe in through your nose (inspiration) till you can't anymore and then breathe out through your mouth (expiration). It has a way of bringing me to my centre. It took me a long time to understand these simple truths and as a result, I became prone to very low self-esteem, low self-confidence, which made me pessimistic. That is why we will do the opposite ladies and gentlemen; we are going to live and live the kind of lives that we will be proud of first by being true and understanding who we truly are and where it is that we want to go.

Finding yourself is worth pursuing no matter the cost because it brings us to alertness about ourselves that can only make us greater. Right at the beginning of the book, I implored all my readers to find an identity that is independent of anyone, your lover, your friends, your parents, your family, your religion, and I am repeating this. Once you make decisions and forge identities based on other people's expectations of you, it becomes only a matter of time before the house of cards comes crashing down.

I once knew an intelligent young man who went to one of the most prestigious private schools in South Africa and whose life had already been mapped out by his parents. He was an all-rounder, straight-A student, first-team rugby, debating team, chess player, water polo, you name it, and he was even a prefect. He was always so eager to please that I think pleasing his teachers and his parents came at a great cost to him. A cost he also would not fully understand until he reached university. He got accepted into medical school and his parents had never been prouder. I don't think he wanted to be a doctor, but because all his marks and accolades were able to get him into medical school, he went along anyway and just prayed that this would work itself out and that he would become a doctor for his parents.

Before the end of the second semester, he was an inpatient at a mental institution and would have to stay for six months as various diagnoses were made and different treatments were instituted. He was only nineteen years old. I had explained earlier that the mind attacks. If your entire life was lived for other people there is a time where the mind gets tired of putting on a mask every day and when it attacks, it causes a tsunami type of effect as it begins not to attack a foreign entity like bacteria as in Meningitis, but it forms a planned and deadly attack against self and this pursuit of your truth suddenly becomes an emergency.

There can only be so many triggers before the protective factors in your life such as a great support system stop assisting your overall prognosis. Do not wait until a tsunami of the mind stops you in your tracks. Find the strength to own up to your truth sooner.

The young man recovered and is now a graphic designer at the start of his career. The parents had to let go of the unrealistic expectations that they had set for him and allow him to live and seek out his happiness. That magical word happiness. By living your truth and forging an identity something miraculous happens, happiness comes knocking bearing gifts of hope, love, determination, renewed and heightened self-confidence, self-compassion, healthy boundaries, and healthy decisions on sound career paths. An awareness of where it is that you want to go and then by the smallest steps, you reach those beautiful destinations. Do not forget to celebrate those milestones on your journey to finding yourself. Here is the truth about comfort zones, "A comfort zone is a beautiful place, but nothing grows there." Gina Milicia.

Resilience is often defined as the process of adapting well in the face of adversity, trauma, tragedy, and other myriads of afflictions that are a consequence of being alive. It's usually termed as the process of bouncing back and the ability to recover after immense trauma. It is linked to finding meaning as most of the things that bring all sorts of grief to our door must be processed and resilience is a big part that goes along the five stages of grief. Finding meaning is the final ingredient that not only changes our perspective of the trauma but also makes it meaningful in that we can carry on. It is my hope and prayer that we find ourselves and strive every day to live more meaningful lives. As we do this so much of our lives fall into place and we become the versions of ourselves we were created to become. B'ezrat HaShem (with God's help), you will achieve all your dreams.

I will leave you with this beautiful Ramcharitmanas Siddha mantra[18] in Hindi to help you find the correct path to success. Chant this mantra for success with great faith and devotion.

> *"Jehi vidhi hoi naath hit moraa karahu so vegi daas main toraa."*
>
> *"O, Lord, I don't know what to do,*
> *I don't know which direction to go.*
> *I hereby surrender to you, to your will, and*
> *I know you will do whatever is good for me."*

ABOUT THE AUTHOR

D r Zikhona Hlalempini is a mother of four beautiful children—three boys and a princess. She lives and works in East London and is currently in private practice as a Family Practitioner. She holds degrees in both Medicine and Dietetics. Her main interests are in mental health advocacy, geriatrics, and household food security. Her main aim in life is to ensure that the majority of South Africans understand these key concepts. When she is not consulting with her clients or writing, she spends her free time painting, playing chess with her children, and gardening, where she plants the vegetables, they consume at home. She is an avid reader who reads most genres but is still stuck on the classics—an addiction that still draws her back to TS Elliot's The Wasteland whenever life seems a little dull. She hopes to be an agent of change in the ever-evolving world we live in. She currently engages and welcomes public speaking engagements and renders her coaching services as part of attaining her goal of getting South Africans to be more aware of their destinies and the power that their dreams hold in shaping their futures. She hopes to teach that, through self-identity and hard work, it is possible to reach all your goals. She wants you to know that you can live the life that you hope to live, that It Can Turn for everyone.

REFERENCES

1   McCullough, C. (1977). *The Thorn Birds*. Harper & Row

2   Dickinson, E. (1896). Love, Poem 16: Apocalypse. The Poems of Emily Dickinson: Series One (Lit2Go Edition). Retrieved August 2021 from https://etc.usf.edu/lit2go/114/the-poems-of-emily-dickinson-series-one/2394/love-poem-16-apocalypse

3   Yolen, J. (1981). *Touch Magic: Fantasy, Faeri & Folklore in the Literature of Childhood*. Philomel Books.

4   Plath, S. (2000). *The Unabridged Journals of Sylvia Plath*. Anchor

5   Kaufman, C. E. (1998). Contraceptive use in South Africa under Apartheid. *Demography, 35*(4), 421-434

6   Bhuda, G. B., & Sekudu, J. (2016). Abortion and Contraceptives: An Exploratory Study. *Southern African Journal of Social Work and Social Development, 28*(2), 122-137.

7   Rothfuss, P. (2007). *The name of the wind*. New York: Penguin Group DAW

8   Gontsana, M. (2014). Games that township kids play. GroundUp. Retrieved in August 2021 from https://www.groundup.org.za/article/games-township-kids-play_2450/

9   Lord Tennyson, A. From the Princess: Tears, Idle Tears. Retrieved in August 2021 from https://www.poetryfoundation.org/poems/45384/the-princess-tears-idle-tears

10 Pound, E. (1915) The River-Merchant's Wife: A Letter. Retrieved August 2021. https://www.poetryfoundation.org/poems/47692/the-river-merchants-wife-a-letter-56d22853677f9

11 Bishop, E. (1979). One Art from The Complete Poems 1926-1979 (Farrar, Strauss, and Giroux, 1983)

12 Dickinson, E. (1924). The complete poems of Emily Dickinson. Boston. Retrieved August 2021. https://www.bartleby.com/113/3002.html

13 Farreras, I. G. (2013). History of Mental Illness. *Noba textbook series: Psychology.* Retrieved August 2021. https://nobaproject.com/modules/history-of-mental-illness

14 Gillis, L. (2012). The historical development of psychiatry in South Africa since 1652. *South African Journal of Psychiatry*, 18 (3), 78-82.

15 Ehrmann, M. (1927). Desiderata. Retrieved in August 2021 from https://www.desiderata.com/desiderata.html

16 Mqhayi, S. E. K. (1943). Sinking of the Mendi. *Inzuzo.* Johannesburg: Wits University Press. Retrieved in August 2021 from https://www.poetryinternational.org/pi/poem/13291/auto/0/0/SEK-Mqhayi/SINKING-OF-THE-MENDI/en/tile

17 Bryant, W. C. (1817). Thanatopsis. North American Review. Retrieved in August from https://www.poetryfoundation.org/poems/50465/thanatopsis

18 Mantra to find correct path for success in Hindi. Retrieved in August 2021 from http://www.hindugodganesh.com/mantra/ramcharitmanas-siddha-mantra

www.ingramcontent.com/pod-product-compliance
Lightning Source LLC
Chambersburg PA
CBHW030828090426
42737CB00009B/915